Business and Management Internships

Research shows that internships are the dominant form of experiential learning used in business schools worldwide, providing practical insight into a job role for students and enhancing their employability.

This book provides practical resources that practitioners and students can use to maximize the overall internship experience by explaining business education, internships, skill development, and employment outcomes. It also includes material to assist in the development or enhancement of internship programs to create a high-quality internship course while providing guidance on reflecting and evaluating the learning gained from the experience. Including quizzes and short activities, this book can be used as a companion text for any student participating in an internship, or as a guide that practitioners in this field can use to help design their own internship program and course content.

Business schools are increasing their focus on experiential learning and are encouraging faculty to incorporate internships into their existing curriculum. Linking theory, history, and practice, this book is ideal reading for students participating in an internship for academic credit and as a guidebook for business school practitioners who wish to start or improve their existing academic internship program.

Kawana W. Johnson serves as the director of Internships & Career Services/Teaching Faculty in the Florida State University College of Business where she oversees the internship office and serves as instructor of record for the online internship courses.

Business and Management Internships

Improving Employability through Experiential Learning

Kawana W. Johnson

LONDON AND NEW YORK

First published 2022
by Routledge
2 Park Square, Milton Park, Abingdon, Oxon OX14 4RN

and by Routledge
605 Third Avenue, New York, NY 10158

Routledge is an imprint of the Taylor & Francis Group, an informa business

© 2022 Kawana W. Johnson

The right of Kawana W. Johnson to be identified as author of this work has been asserted by her in accordance with sections 77 and 78 of the Copyright, Designs and Patents Act 1988.

All rights reserved. No part of this book may be reprinted or reproduced or utilised in any form or by any electronic, mechanical, or other means, now known or hereafter invented, including photocopying and recording, or in any information storage or retrieval system, without permission in writing from the publishers.

Trademark notice: Product or corporate names may be trademarks or registered trademarks, and are used only for identification and explanation without intent to infringe.

British Library Cataloguing-in-Publication Data
A catalogue record for this book is available from the British Library

Library of Congress Cataloging-in-Publication Data
Names: Johnson, Kawana W., 1979- author.
Title: Business and management internships : improving employability through experiential learning/Kawana W. Johnson.
Description: First Edition. | New York : Routledge, 2021. | Includes bibliographical references and index. |
Identifiers: LCCN 2021002942 (print) | LCCN 2021002943 (ebook) | ISBN 9780367493318 (hardback) | ISBN 9780367493332 (paperback) | ISBN 9781003045779 (ebook)
Subjects: LCSH: Business education (Internship) | Business education. | Management--Study and teaching. | Experiential learning.
Classification: LCC HF1106 .J544 2021 (print) | LCC HF1106 (ebook) | DDC 658.3/1243--dc23
LC record available at https://lccn.loc.gov/2021002942
LC ebook record available at https://lccn.loc.gov/2021002943

ISBN: 978-0-367-49331-8 (hbk)
ISBN: 978-0-367-49333-2 (pbk)
ISBN: 978-1-003-04577-9 (ebk)

Typeset in Bembo
by MPS Limited, Dehradun

This book is dedicated to my family, friends, students, and the many colleagues that pour themselves into this important work on a daily basis! Through much faith, support, and hard work, this project has come to fruition.

Contents

List of Illustrations	ix
About the Author	x
Preface	xi

1 History of Business Education   1

The Early Years 1
Conclusion 6
References 7

2 Internships and Their Impact on Business Education   9

Impact 9
Benefits and Limitations 10
International and Virtual Internships 12
Internships from a Theoretical Perspective 13
Conclusion 16
References 17

3 The Skills Gap   21

Skills Gap Defined 21
Generational Impact 22
Skills for the Future 23
Conclusion 28
References 29

4 Ideas and Strategies for a Successful Internship Program   31

Introduction 31
Using Existing Institutional Technology 31
Engage with Employers 34
Recruit Student Ambassadors 37
Your Local Business Community 37
Communicate and Recognize 39

Other Events and Activities 43
Programs that Promote Diversity and Inclusion 50
Conclusion 52
References 52

5 Internship Courses in a Changing Environment 53

Introduction 53
Instructional Delivery Methods 54
Academic Internship Course Defined 55
Online Internship Course Design 57
Timelines & Flexibility 60
Using Modules in Your Learning Management System 60
Assignments 62
Alternative Internship Course Design 68
Conclusion 71
References 71

6 The Future of Business Education and Employment 73

The Future of Business Education 73
Employment Outlook 76
Internships and their Role in Employment 77
Internships During COVID-19 77
Conclusion 78
References 78

Appendices 81

Appendix A	Sample Internship Course Enrollment Application (Online Form) 82
Appendix B	Sample Employer Internship Confirmation (Online Form) 84
Appendix C	Sample Internship Course Syllabus Outline 86
Appendix D	Sample Course Outline – Learning Experientially in Business 89
Appendix E	Sample Assignments and Rubrics 92
Appendix F	Sample Employer Midterm Evaluation (Online Form) 96
Appendix G	Sample Employer Final Evaluation (Online Form) 97

Index 99

List of Illustrations

Figure

2.1 Constructivist Theories of Learning   13

Tables

3.1 Identify and Execute   27
3.2 Skills Analysis   28
5.1 Credit Hour Summary   56
5.2 Grading Plan   59
5.3 Point Value Summary   59
5.4 Sample Course Modules   61
C.1 Sample Course Outline   87
D.1 Sample Course Outline – Learning Experientially in Business   89
E.1 Assignment #1 Sample Rubric   92
E.2 Assignment #2 Sample Rubric   92
E.3 Assignment #3 Sample Rubric   93
E.4 Assignment #4 Sample Rubric   94
E.5 Assignment #5 Sample Rubric   94
F.1 Sample Midterm Employer Evaluation   96
G.1 Sample Employer Final Evaluation   97

About the Author

Kawana W. Johnson is the director of Internships and Career Services in the Florida State University College of Business where she holds a teaching faculty designation. In this role, she oversees the daily operations of the office, assists students in finding internship opportunities, and serves as instructor for the college's online internship courses. She has more than 17 years of experience in higher education and extensive knowledge in career services, experiential learning, and workforce development. She is a graduate of Troy University, with a bachelor of science in broadcast journalism and public relations; Florida State University, with a master of science in higher education; and the University of South Florida, with a Ph.D. in career and workforce education.

Preface

This book emerged from several years of lessons learned as an intern, career services professional, internship director, and faculty member responsible for internship course development. Each role was a building block that gave me the experience I needed to advance toward the next "thing." Fortunately, I'm not finished adding blocks of experience to my journey and you shouldn't be either. This book is another resource to help students make the most of their internship experience while giving the practitioner a tool to help develop or expand their own internship program and course. Internships are one of the most popular forms of experiential learning used in business schools worldwide. With this knowledge comes an increased need for academia to develop quality programs while providing students with a structured approach to gain the most out of their own experiences.

This book provides practical resources that practitioners and students can use to maximize the overall internship experience. As you begin this book, keep several things in mind. The material is divided into six chapters. While all chapters can be useful to both students and practitioners, chapter 4 and 5 were written with the practitioner in mind. The material between those pages should assist the practitioner in developing or enhancing an internship program and creating a quality online internship course. The remaining chapters provide the reader with a better understanding of business education, internships, skill development, employment outcomes, and the future of the discipline. Chapter 1–3 include quizzes and/or short activities to ensure that students gain a solid grasp of the material presented. As with any internship course, this book is reflective in nature with chapters that can be used as a companion text for any student participating in an internship course or as a guide that practitioners in this field can use to help design their own internship program and course content.

If you are serious about taking your internship experience or program to the next level, this book may be the resource you need. I wish you the best in your journey and encourage you to never stop learning!

1 History of Business Education

"Those who don't know history are doomed to repeat it."

Edmund Burke

The Early Years

For many, the name "Wharton" symbolizes prestige, superiority, and excellence in business education. That symbolism is rightfully placed with its identification as the formal establishment of undergraduate business education in the United States (Hugstad 1983). Since the founding of the Wharton School at the University of Pennsylvania in 1881, undergraduate business education has seen tremendous growth. By 1924, 117 colleges and schools of business existed (Hayes & Jackson, 1935), and by 2011 that number grew to more than 13,000 (Fernandes, 2011). Between World War I and World War II, large corporations were developed, business and social status became more intertwined, and women were granted access to business education representing 17% of business degrees by 1928 (Hugstad, 1983). Over the years, the study of business progressed from a trade to a rigorous and respected profession that was formally introduced to Historically Black Colleges and Universities (HBCUs) in the 1930s (Jackson, Davis, & Harvey, 2019). By 1950, business school education had produced more than 76,000 baccalaureate degrees and more than 363,799 by 2015, making business one of the most popular degree programs in the nation (Kensing, 2013; National Center for Education Statistics, 2016).

Gordon-Howell Report

In the 1950s, a period of "self-criticism and examination" (Hugstad, 1983, p. 10) of the business school led to the development of two landmark studies, *The Education of American Businessmen: A Study of University-College Programmes in Business Administration* by Professor Frank C. Pierson and *Higher Education for Business* by economists Robert A. Gordon and James E. Howell ("Gordon-Howell," 2009; Schoemaker, 2008; Zimmerman, 2001). These studies, funded by the Carnegie Foundation and the Ford Foundation, respectively, addressed concerns among critics citing uncertainty about the future of business education and its overall impact ("Gordon-Howell," 2009; Schoemaker, 2008; Zimmerman, 2001). Of the two reports, the Ford Foundation study, led by economists Robert A. Gordon and James E. Howell *(later known as the Gordon-Howell Report),* were the most dismal, prompting their reference to business education as an assembly of vocational schools with narrow curriculum; ineffective staff; low-quality students; and a faculty that focused more on consulting than research, theory, and ethics ("Gordon-Howell," 2009; Hugstad, 1983; Schoemaker, 2008; Zimmerman, 2001). The effects of this report were felt in business schools around the world and scholars began suggesting that business education do a better job focusing on the student's entire career and not just the first job (Zimmerman, 2001). Overall, the Gordon-Howell Report produced in-depth research while providing more than $30 million to address business education reform (Morsing & Rovira, 2011; Schlossman, Sedlak, & Wechsler, 1987).

The recommendations included an increase in the general education content of undergraduate studies, elimination of concentrations and streamlining of the number of required courses, a shift in teaching methods, and higher standards in the student admission process (Gordon & Howell, 1959). In addition, scholars believed that more faculty with doctorate degrees in the social sciences and quantitative fields where necessary to increase training in quantitative analysis and the behavioral sciences (Morsing & Rovira, 2011). At that time, corporate managers used elaborate quantitative tools developed during the war to run their companies; therefore, it was important to ensure that business graduates were equipped with these skills (Morsing & Rovira, 2011). This approach caused business educators to focus more attention on technical expertise and less on developing socially aware graduates (Morsing & Rovira, 2011). The *Gordon-Howell Report* contributed to substantial changes in business education between 1960 and 1980, causing the discipline to became a more valued component of higher education (Porter & McKibbin, 1988).

Porter McKibbin Report

Almost 30 years later, the Association to Advance Collegiate Schools of Business (AACSB), the world's largest business education alliance, commissioned another study to examine the future of management education from a more holistic view (Association to Advance Collegiate Schools of Business, 2017; Porter & McKibbin, 1988). The *Porter McKibbin Report*, one of the most comprehensive studies of management education to date, identified complacency as the primary barrier that business schools face in their efforts to successfully move into the 21st century (Dalton, Earley, Hitt, & Porter, 2009). This study furthered the findings from the *Gordon-Howell Report* and shed light on the need to bring more attention to developing student skills and other personal characteristics (Porter & McKibbin, 1988). What made this study unique is the inclusion of viewpoints from corporations and third-party providers, areas that Gordon and Howell predicted would play a significant role in business education in the years ahead (Porter & McKibbin, 1988). In the *Porter McKibbin Report*, deans and faculty saw a wide gap in skill development while student perception was in conflict possibly due to their overall lack of work experience (Porter & McKibbin, 1988). Human resource professionals and other corporate employees reported the same concerns and strongly suggested that the business curriculum be enhanced to address these issues (Porter & McKibbin, 1988).

Accreditation

In the early 1900s, educational practices were scrutinized causing a systematic re-evaluation of the mission, values, and benefits of business education. The Association to Advance Collegiate Schools of Business (AACSB) was established in 1916 to address these concerns and promote higher education for business worldwide (Association to Advance Collegiate Schools of Business, 2017; Hayes & Jackson, 1935). Today, AACSB remains the oldest accrediting organization for business schools worldwide and has long been considered the highest level of business school accreditation with only 25% of business schools in the United States achieving this status (All Business Schools, 2017; Shiffler & Bowen, 2015).

The first set of AACSB business school standards was developed in 1919, and throughout the years, multiple updates have been made to meet the needs of the changing business education environment. To date, the most significant changes occurred in 1991, 2003, and 2013 (Miles, Franklin, Heriot, Hadley, & Hazeldine, 2014). The 2013 standards identified three themes for improvement: innovation, impact, and engagement (Association to Advance Collegiate Schools of Business, 2016; Kosnik, Tingle, & Blanton, 2013; Miles et al., 2014). The new standards suggest that business school's experiment with new teaching methods; demonstrate how their institution and students are positively impacting business and society; and incorporate more real-world experiences into the curriculum (Kosnik et al., 2013).

AACSB accredited schools are required to participate in a self-evaluation and a peer review to ensure that they uphold standards that fall under the following four categories: (a) strategic management and innovation; (b) students, faculty, and professional staff; (c) learning and teaching; and (d) academic and professional engagement (Association to Advance Collegiate Schools of Business, 2016; Dumond & Johnson, 2013). Standard #13 specifically addresses the need for business schools to provide experiential learning opportunities.

> For any teaching and learning model employed, the school provides a portfolio of experiential learning opportunities for business students, through either formal coursework or extracurricular activities, which allow them to engage with faculty and active business leaders. These experiential learning activities provide exposure to business and management in both local and global contexts …. They … may include field trips, internships, consulting projects, field research, interdisciplinary projects, extracurricular activities, etc. (Association to Advance Collegiate Schools of Business, 2016, p. 38)

The 2013 standards also included the AACSB core values – ethical behavior among students, faculty, and administrators; a collegial environment; and a commitment toward social responsibility – as requirements for accreditation (Miles et al., 2014). These changes were significant for business schools around the world, prompting deans to re-evaluate their mission, their business relationships, and their strategies for delivery of a quality business education curriculum to the students they serve.

The new standards brought about positive change to individuals and their ability to have their opinions considered; yet deans faced more pressure than ever to shape the culture of their business school while acquiring more external funding to support new initiatives (Miles et al., 2014). In addition, a number of opponents have questioned the value that AACSB accreditation brings to business education (Dumond & Johnson, 2013). Some of those concerns include its suitability for the competitive nature of business education; its role in hindering the schools in their ability to adapt to change but maintain the status quo; and questions regarding whether it works for or against professionalism (Julian & Ofori-Dankwa, 2006; Pfeffer & Fong, 2002; Trank & Rynes, 2003). Advocates cite the value it places on quality and advances in business education; the clear distinction between purpose and strategy; and the external endorsement that it provides to prospective students, faculty, and employers (Romero, 2008; Zammuto, 2008; & Trapnell, 2007). Further research is needed to elaborate on the overall impact of these changes. However, Miles et al. (2014) found the standards to be flexible enough to potentially enhance the global influence of business education for years to come.

Other prominent business accrediting organizations include the Association of Collegiate Business Schools and Programs (ACBSP) and the International Assembly for Collegiate Business Education (IACBE) (Roller, Andrews, & Bovee, 2003). The Accreditation Council for Business Schools and Programs (2017) was established in 1988, with a focus on "recognizing teaching excellence, determining student learning outcomes, and a continuous improvement model" (Accreditation Council for Business Schools and Programs, 2017, para. 1). AACSB and ACBSP both value research, but ACBSP also places a strong focus on the quality of instructional methods (Bennett, Geringer, & Taylor, 2015). Of the three accrediting organizations mentioned, ACBSP is the only one to develop a process to accredit two-year business programs at community colleges and for-profit universities, sectors that account for more than half of their membership base (Bennett, Geringer, & Taylor, 2015; Roller, Andrews, & Bovee, 2003).

The International Assembly for Collegiate Business Education (IACBE) was established in 1997 to evaluate business schools on outcome-based measurements (Bennett, Geringer, & Taylor, 2015). Bennett, Geringer, and Taylor (2015) found that many academicians were concerned that accreditation was too highly focused on research and teaching yet failed to recognize schools with institutional missions that addressed outcomes and results. Institutions that gravitate toward membership in IACBE are typically non-traditional programs and others that failed to meet the accreditation criteria outlined by AACSB or ACBSP. Despite the accrediting body, all ensure that institutions of higher education adhere to high-quality standards based on research and professional practice (All Business Schools, 2017).

Business Education Curriculum

The primary disciplines found in undergraduate schools of business include accounting, finance, management, and marketing (Colby, Ehrlich, Sullivan, & Dolle, 2011). These disciplines have evolved over the years, with an emphasis on scientific knowledge and a close relationship to MBA programs, which explains why many faculty members teach both undergraduate and graduate courses (Colby, Ehrlich, Sullivan, & Dolle, 2011). The core business curriculum was designed to equip students with the skills necessary to function in business; however, early reform initiatives sought to incorporate more liberal arts courses in an effort to strengthen the curriculum (Colby, Ehrlich, Sullivan, & Dolle, 2011).

The early curriculum was extensive, covering everything from political science to sociology and business subjects totaling 91 course topics and 6,624 class hours (Bossard & Dewhurst, 1931; Hayes & Jackson, 1935). Much emphasis was placed on English, but little on courses that covered the fundamentals of business (Bossard & Dewhurst, 1931). The *Gordon-Howell Report* led to major curriculum changes between 1960 and 1980 (Porter & McKibbin, 1988). The recommendations from the report, the Ford Foundation's financial support, and the revised (AACSB) curriculum standards all played a significant role in the change in direction of business education during this era (Porter & McKibbin, 1988). Thus, 50% of the curriculum was directed toward general education, professional core courses were identified, and electives from both business and non-business areas were permitted (Jones, 1984; Porter & McKibbin, 1988).

The *Gordon-Howell Report* also recommended that the role of establishing and enforcing curriculum guidelines is the responsibility of the AACSB (Jones, 1984). Reactions to these suggestions were mixed across the business education community; however, change came swiftly and continues to occur in business schools across the country.

Perhaps the *Gordon-Howell Report* was the impetus for the AACSB's decision to commission another study on the future of management education led by Professors Lyman Porter and Lawrence McKibbin. The *Porter-McKibbin Report* described the current state of management education and elaborated on how it must change for the field to thrive in the years ahead. This report was unique because of the rich perspectives received from both the academic and business community (Porter & McKibbin, 1988). Porter and McKibbin (1988) found seven areas in the curriculum that received harsh criticism. Those areas include:

- An imbalance in the delivery of quantitative vs. qualitative analytical techniques;
- Inadequate attention on how to manage people;
- Lack of attention on developing communication skills;
- Inadequate attention on developing relationships and learning how to cope with the external environment;
- Lack of attention on the international aspects of business;
- Insufficient focus on entrepreneurship; and
- Inadequate attention toward developing ethical business leaders (Porter & McKibbin, 1988).

Additional findings from the *Porter-McKibbin Report* identified business communication, entrepreneurship, international business/management, and management information systems as content areas in need of emphasis while the development of skills and personal characteristics were highlighted as areas in need of special attention (Porter & McKibbin, 1988). Deans and faculty members saw a wide gap in skill development while student perception was in conflict, possibly due to their overall lack of work experience (Porter & McKibbin, 1988). Human resource professionals and other corporate employees reported the same concerns and strongly suggested that the business curriculum be enhanced to address these issues (Porter & McKibbin, 1988).

Jones (1984) identified major concerns with the structure of the postsecondary business education curriculum in the areas of course design, credibility of sources and components used in course development, and career preparation and employment outcomes. These issues forced some scholars to believe that the new curriculum failed to produce graduates that were equipped with the tools necessary to handle real-life business situations. Instead, graduates were leaving their institutions able to perform calculations but lacking in skills to manage others (Jones, 1984). A debate was also ignited on whether material taught in business schools should come from the faculty, students, business, or society (Jones, 1984). With many schools relying on faculty to determine course content and research areas, critics noted that such a contained system could stifle the development of successful business school graduates (Jones, 1984).

6 History of Business Education

Conclusion

Regardless of the industry or the role you occupy, business impacts every area of our lives and is a necessary form of education in a thriving economy. Due to the changing economy, industry professionals now expect business students to come into the workforce job-ready. Therefore, the responsibility comes back to academia to prepare students theoretically and experientially with the skills to make wise decisions and handle business situations as they arise (Kumar & Bhandarker, 2017). With this knowledge comes a gradual shift in the priorities of business education to ensure that curriculum is more relevant to the changing demographics, employer satisfaction is taken into consideration (Eisner, 1999; Hodge et al., 2014; Jones, 1984), and standards are periodically "modified to emphasize quality and continuous improvement in the changing collegiate business education environments" (Miles, Franklin, Heriot, Hadley, & Hazeldine, 2014, p. 87).

Chapter Quiz
1. What is considered the world's first collegiate business school in the United States?
2. Which remains the oldest accrediting organization for business schools worldwide and has long been considered the highest level of business school accreditation?
3. Name the two other prominent business school accrediting organizations discussed in this chapter.
4. Which report, funded by the Carnegie Foundation, produced in-depth research on business education, resulting in more than $30 million to address business education reform?
5. Which report was commissioned by the AACSB in 1988 and furthered earlier findings on business education?
6. The early business school curriculum was extensive, covering everything from political science to sociology and business subjects totaling how many course topics and class hours?
7. The *Porter McKibbin Report* found seven areas in the business curriculum that received harsh criticisms. Identify those areas.

Quiz Answers:
1. The Wharton School at the University of Pennsylvania
2. The Association to Advance Collegiate Schools of Business (AACSB)
3. The Association of Collegiate Business Schools and Programs (ACBSP) and The International Assembly for Collegiate Business Education (IACBE)
4. The *Gordon-Howell Report* of 1959
5. The *Porter McKibbin Report*
6. 91 course topics and 6,624 class hours
7.
    - An imbalance in the delivery of quantitative vs. qualitative analytical techniques;
    - Inadequate attention on how to manage people;
    - Lack of attention on developing communication skills;
    - Inadequate attention on developing relationships and learning how to cope with the external environment;
    - Lack of attention on the international aspects of business;
    - Insufficient focus on entrepreneurship; and
    - Inadequate attention toward developing ethical business leaders

References

Accreditation Council for Business Schools & Programs. (2017). *Discover ACBSP*. https://www.acbsp.org/page/about_us?

All Business Schools. (2017). *Business School Accreditation*. Retrieved from https://www.allbusinessschools.com/business-administration/common-questions/business-school-accreditation/

Association to Advance Collegiate Schools of Business. (2017). *About us*. Retrieved from www.aacsb.edu/about

Bennett, P. J., Geringer, S. D., Taylor, J. (2015). The effect of accreditation on the university selection of undergraduate business majors: An empirical study. *International Journal of Education Research*. Retrieved from https://www.thefreelibrary.com/ The effect of accreditation on the university selection of...-a0417473395

Bossard, J. H. S. & Dewhurst, J.F. (1931). *University education for business*. Philadelphia, PA: University of Pennsylvania Press.

Caulfield, J. & Woods, T. (2013). Experiential learning: Exploring its long-term impact on socially responsible behavior. *Journal of the Scholarship of Teaching and Learning*, 13(2), 31–48.

Colby, A. Ehrlich, T, Sullivan, W. M. & Dolle, J. R. (2011). *Rethinking undergraduate business education: Liberal learning for the profession*. San Francisco: Jossey-Bass.

College Atlas. (2014). *Association to Advance Collegiate Schools of Business (AACSB)*. Retrieved from https://www.collegeatlas.org/association-to-advance-collegiate-schools- of-business.html

Dalton, D. R., Earley, P. C., Hitt, M. A., Porter, L. W. (2009, August). Revisiting the Porter-McKibbin Report: Where do we stand, and where are we going? In P. M. Podsakoff & N. P. Podsakoff (Chairs), *Green Management Matters*. Symposium conducted at the annual meeting of the Academy of Management, Chicago, IL.

Dumond, E. J., & Johnson, T. W. (2013). Managing university business educational quality: ISO or AACSB. *Quality Assurance in Education*, 21(2), 127–144.

Eisner, S. (1999). The impact of business school on student attitudes towards diversity in the 21st century workplace. *Transformations*, 10(1), 49. Retrieved from https://login.proxy.lib.fsu.edu/login?url=http://search.proquest.com/docview/220383150?accountid=4840

Fernandes, J. (2011, November/December). Big Questions. *BizEd X*(6), 60–65.

Gordon, R., & Howell, J. (1959). *Higher education for business*. New York: Columbia University Press.

Gordon-Howell Report of 1959: The more things change ... (2009). *The Economist*. Retrieved from http://www.economist.com/node/12762453

Grair, C. A. (2007). Experiential learning in business German workshops. *Global Business Languages*, 7(8), 1–21. Retrieved from http://docs.lib.purdue.edu/gbl/vol7/iss1/8

Hayes, B. R. & Jackson, H. P. (1935). *A history of business education in the United States*. Cincinnati, Ohio: Southwestern Publishing.

Hergert, M. (2009). Student perceptions of the value of internships in business education. *American Journal of Business Education*, 2(8), 9–13.

Hodge, L., Proudford, K. L. & Holt, H. (2014). From periphery to core: The increasing relevance of experiential learning in undergraduate business education. *Research in Higher Education Journal*, 26, 1–17.

Hugsted, P. S. (1983). *The business schools in the 1980s: Liberalism versus vocationalism*. New York: Praeger Publishers.

Jackson, A. J. , Davis, E. L. , & Harvey, B. H. (2019). *Business education and historically black colleges and universities*. Retrieved from https://www.aacsb.edu/insights/2019/March/business-education-and-historically-black-colleges-and-universities#gsc.tab=0

Jones, C. G. (1984). *A descriptive study of a business school curriculum design as it relates to the skill and knowledge needs of recent graduates*. (Doctoral dissertation). University of South Carolina, Columbia, South Carolina.

Julian, S. & Ofori-Dankwa, J. (2006). Is accreditation good for the strategic decision making of traditional business schools? *Academy of Management Learning and Education, 5*(3), 225–233.

Kensing, K. (2013, July). College majors and employment trends. *CareerCast.com.* Retrieved from http://www.careercast.com/career-news/college-majors-employment-trends

Kosnik, R. D., Tingle, J. K., & Blanton, E. L. (2013). Transformational learning in business education: The pivotal role of experiential learning projects. *American Journal of Business Education, 6*(6), 615–630.

Kumar, S. & Bhandarker, A. (2017). Experiential learning and its relevance in business school curriculum. *Developments in Business Simulation and Experiential Learning, 44,* 244–251.

Miles, M. P., Franklin, G. M., Heriot, K., Hadley, L., & Hazeldine, M. (2014). AACSB International's 2013 accreditation standards: Speculative implications for faculty and Stadeans. *Journal of International Education in Business, 7*(2), 85–107.

Morsing, M. & Rovira, A. S. (2011). *Business schools and their contribution to society.* Los Angeles, CA: SAGE.

National Center for Education Statistics. (2016). *Fast facts.* Retrieved from https://nces.ed.gov/fastfacts/display.asp?id=37

Pfeffer, J. & Fong, C. T. (2002). The end of business schools? Less success than meets the eye. *Academy of Management Learning & Education, 1*(1), 78–95.

Porter, L. W. & McKibbin, L. E. (1988). *Management education and development: Drift or thrust into the 21st century?* New York: McGraw-Hill Book Company.

Roller, Andrews, and Bovee (2003). Specialized accreditation of business schools: A comparison of alternative costs, benefits, and motivations. *Journal of Education for Business, 4*(78), 197–204.

Romero, E. (2008). AACSB accreditation: Addressing faculty concerns. *Academy of Management Learning and Education, 7*(2), 245–255.

Schlossman, S., Sedlak, M., & Wechsler, H. (1987). The "new look"; the Ford Foundation and the revolution in business education. *Selections: The Magazine of the Graduate Management Admission Council, 14*(3), 8–28.

Schoemaker, P. J. H. (2008). The future challenges of business: Rethinking management education. *California Management Review, 50*(3), 119–139.

Shiffler, R. E. & Bowen, H. P. (2015). Peers, aspirants and competitors: Developing a set of comparison schools for AACSB Accreditation Reviews. *Academy of Educational Leadership Journal, 19*(2), 135–142.

Trank, C. & Rynes, S. (2003). Who moved our cheese? Reclaiming professionalism in business Education. *Academy of Management Learning and Education, 2,*189–205.

Trapnell, J. E. (2007). AACSB International Accreditation – the value proposition and a look to the future. *Journal of Management Development, 26*(1), 67–72.

USA Today. (2016). *Same as it ever was: Top 10 most popular college majors.* Retrieved from http://college.usatoday.com/2014/10/26/same-as-it-ever-was-top-10-most-popular-college-majors/

Zammuto, R. F. (2008). Accreditation and the globalization of business. *Academy of Management Learning & Education, 7,* 256–268.

Zimmerman, J. L. (2001). *Can American business schools survive?* (Working Paper No. FR 01-16). Retrieved from the Social Science Research Network website: http://papers.ssrn.com/abstract=283112

2 Internships and Their Impact on Business Education

"Tell me and I forget, teach me and I may remember, involve me and I learn"

Benjamin Franklin

Impact

Business schools have a long history of focusing on preparing students conceptually, theoretically, and philosophically to excel in business, government, and social sectors while others prioritize research (Hodge, Proudford, & Holt, 2014). Fortunately, a shift has occurred and more business schools are giving priority to identifying skills employers seek and ensuring that curriculum is regularly re-examined, and taking employer satisfaction into consideration to keep up with the rapidly changing corporate environment (Beard, Schwieger, & Surendran, 2008; Eisner, 1999; Hodge et al., 2014).

To help close the skills gap, many undergraduate business schools have incorporated forms of experiential learning – "learning by doing" – into the curriculum (Caulfield & Woods, 2013; Grair, 2007; Kolb, 2015; Rizk, 2011). The most common forms of experiential learning offered in postsecondary business education include internships, mentorships, service learning, capstone courses, cooperative education placements, job shadowing, and a curriculum based on entrepreneurship (Govekar & Rishi, 2007; Griffis, 2014; McCarthy & McCarthy, 2006). Internships are the most widely used form of experiential learning offered in postsecondary business education (Griffis, 2014; Sciplimpaglia & Toole, 2009). With experiential learning, learners can experience, reflect, think, and act in a "recursive process that is sensitive to the learning situation and what is being learned" (Kolb, 2015, p. 51; Kolb & Kolb, 2009, p. 298). Kolb's learning model serves as a visual representation of how "knowledge is created through the transformation of experience" (Kolb, 2015, p. 49). The experiential learning cycle involves concrete experience *(the learner encounters new experience)*, reflective observation *(learner reflects on that experience)*, abstract conceptualization *(the learner creates new ideas or modifies existing)*, and active experimentation *(the learner puts into action what they have learned)* (Kolb, 2015). This model demonstrates that for effective learning to occur, the learner should complete all four stages.

Over the years, higher education has seen an increase in the use of experiential learning as a training tool. The primary reasons for this increase include (a) the onset of new technologies that provide useful tools for training; (b) younger generations preferring experiential learning over other methods of education; and (c) the belief that creative people bring significant ideas (Silberman, 2007). Scholars have come to the realization that courses alone will not produce long-term, proficient practitioners

(Hager, 2011). Therefore, experiential learning programs provide an educational alternative to help develop and maintain a highly skilled workforce.

Employer demand and an increased push by the Association to Advance Collegiate Schools of Business (AACSB) to increase experiential learning in both local and global practices of business have been significant factors in the growth of experiential learning in postsecondary business education (Griffis, 2014; Hart Research Associates, 2008; Sciglimpaglia & Toole, 2009). A poll by Hart Research Associates (2008) found that employers preferred practical experience to traditional classroom lectures as a method of teaching. Therefore, the need for an enhanced curriculum becomes more evident as business schools work to produce the employees that employers seek while meeting and maintaining the standards that their accrediting agency requires. Research continues to suggest that experiential learning enhances student development and that adults learn more effectively by doing (Fenwick, 2000, 2001, 2003; Kolb & Kolb, 2008). However, Rosenstein, Sweeney, and Gupta (2012), note that a shared language could help schools better understand experiential learning so that its effectiveness transcends programs and majors, thus making it a necessary and vital component in higher education and beyond (Eyler & Giles, 1999; Fenwick, 2000, 2001, 2003; Kolb & Kolb, 2008; Moore, Barry, & Dooley, 2010).

Dr. George Kuh, founding director of the National Institute for Learning Outcomes Assessment, refers to internships as a high impact practice. "High-impact practices, or HIPs, are active learning practices that promote deep learning by promoting student engagement as measured by the National Survey on Student Engagement" (University of Wisconsin Eau Claire, 2020, para 1). "These practices typically demand that students devote considerable time and effort to purposeful tasks; most require daily decisions that deepen students' investment in the activity as well as their commitment to their academic program and the college" (Kuh & Schneider, 2008, p. 24). Research suggest that high-impact practices increase rates of student retention and student engagement (Kuh & O'Donnell, 2013).

Benefits and Limitations

Experiential learning comes in many forms, but internships are the "preferred method of business schools worldwide to give students practical experiences and help them transition to the real world" (Kosnik, Tingle, & Blanton, 2013, p. 616). Internships provide students with an opportunity to explore career options while determining likes and dislikes without sacrificing a significant amount of time (Rothman & Sisman, 2016). As students investigate jobs, they are also able to reflect on their personal needs and interest thereby aiding in their ability to narrow potential career options (Rothman & Sisman, 2016). Many scholars note that internships can clarify job interest; inform students of employer expectations; enlighten students on what they can expect from the job; and assist students in reflecting on whether or not a particular job will be a good fit both personally and professionally (Hiltebeitel, Leauby, & Larkin, 2000; Lord, Sumrall, & Sambandam, 2011; McCarthy & McCarthy, 2006; Rothman, 2007; Moghaddam, 2011). Rothman and Sisman (2016) found that internships have become such a prevalent component of undergraduate education that many scholars believe participation should be mandatory for students enrolled in business schools (Divine, Linrud, Miller, & Wilson, 2007; Hiltebeitel, Leauby, & Larkin, 2000; McCarthy & McCarthy, 2006; Rothman & Sisman, 2016; Templeton, Updyke, & Bennett, 2012).

Alon (2003) noted that several skills are developed as a result of experiential learning including communication, teamwork, problem-solving, and critical thinking. Internships also help students (a) produce stronger resumes, (b) perform better on job interviews, (c) enhance networking skills, (d) gain academic credit, (e) obtain job offers quicker than their peers, and (f) obtain higher starting salaries (Coco, 2000; Divine et al., 2007; Gault, Leach, & Duey, 2010; Knemeyer & Murphy, 2002). Internships allow students to immerse themselves into an organization's culture, participate in realistic tasks, gain insight into career choices, prepare for future employment, gain an individualized experience, and provide motivation to remain in a chosen career field (Divine, Linrud, Miller, & Wilson, 2007; Kosnik, Tingle, & Blanton, 2013). Internships also help students develop skills in judgment, integrity, trust, and collaboration while promoting the development of moral values (Kosnik, Tingle, & Blanton, 2013). Gault, Redington, and Schlager (2000) found that interns have greater job satisfaction and also have more leverage to request a higher salary. When implemented correctly, internships can improve skills and "solve a variety of other workplace issues while offering mutually beneficial outcomes for students, employees, and employers" (Smith, 2015, para 1). Graduating a large volume of students is simply not enough to meet the demands of a changing workforce (Kavas, 2013).

Knouse and Fontenot (2008) found that while internships enhance employability and allow interns to gain both work and organizational learning, they can be improved with clearer expectations, more hands-on experience, and more involvement from both students and employers during the internship development process. "The value of the internship will be maximized if educators can provide the appropriate structure and integrate the experience with the academic background of the student" (Hergert, 2009, p. 12). Business schools are constantly trying to attract the best students and develop relationships with top companies (Gerken, Rienties, Giesbers, & Konings, 2012). Therefore, improvements in the effectiveness of internships can provide significant benefits not only to the students but employers and business schools alike.

Other limitations that internships pose for students and institutions include (a) an extensive time commitment, (b) logistics and location, (c) placement, (d) costs, (e) variableness in the quality of the experience, (f) limited integration with business curriculum, (g) unstructured learning experience, (h) incomplete learning cycle, and (i) less conducive to teamwork (Kosnik, Tingle, & Blanton, 2013). Requiring students to participate in an internship would require administrative expertise, a large network of employers (Divine, Linrud, Miller, & Wilson, 2007), and a dedicated staff to coordinate student assignments which could be very costly to "smaller schools and programs, or for schools located in rural areas" (Kosnik, Tingle, & Blanton, 2013, p. 617).

Updates to AACSB accreditation standards state that schools must "provide a portfolio of experiential learning opportunities for business students, through either formal coursework or extracurricular activities, which allow them to engage with faculty and active business leaders" and ensure these activities "provide exposure to business and management in both local and diverse global contexts" (Association to Advance Collegiate Schools of Business, 2018, p. 42). Experiential learning typifies the AACSB directives of innovation, impact, and engagement while providing students with the opportunity for both personal and professional growth (Kosnik, Tingle, & Blanton, 2013). In addition, Generation Y has shown a preference toward experiential learning as an educational tool, therefore, warranting increased attention on this teaching technique to ensure that learning expectations are addressed and met (Kumar & Bhandarker, 2017).

Bennis and O'Toole (2005) found that business school graduates are not receiving enough training in the skills necessary to compete in the labor market. In fact, "business leaders in the United States and around the world consistently report that they struggle to find skilled, qualified workers to support their customers' needs and keep their companies competitive" (ACT, 2017, p. 2). These findings have elevated internships as a necessary component in the undergraduate business curriculum (Birch et al., 2010; Gault et al., 2000; Hurst & Good, 2010) making them a viable option to help learners cultivate the skills, competencies, and values that generate new ideas and prepare graduates for successful careers (Association to Advance Collegiate Schools of Business, 2016).

International and Virtual Internships

International internships and virtual internships have become popular alternatives to the traditional internships offered in many colleges and schools of business. According to Zhang (2012), trends in globalization have produced a world in need of intercultural competence in communication, work experience, and understanding. Through participation in an international internship, students are able to gain these skills along with a sense of confidence and independence that they may not be able to obtain in an internship located in their home country (Zhang, 2012).

Unfortunately, international internships present financial and physical constraints for some students creating a space to introduce virtual internships into the curriculum. The increase in online learning and the growing effects of these constraints have contributed to an increase in the development of virtual internships in higher education (Ruggiero & Boehm, 2016). Virtual internships help to "equip the student with the necessary skills for teleworking and online collaboration in an international setting, skills that he or she will most likely need more and more in his or her future professional life" (Vriens, 2015, p. 63). Virtual internships also provide more flexibility in work schedules, but often leave the intern feeling isolated when working on a large project with clearly defined goals (Vriens, 2015). Acknowledging these limitations allows the supervisor to set agreements with the intern to establish consistent communication and tools to aid in collaboration throughout the virtual experience (Vriens, 2015). In addition, Vriens (2015) notes that having interaction with multiple employees of a company during a virtual internship helps the student develop socialization skills and cultural competence.

During the coronavirus pandemic (COVID-19), the world saw a surge in virtual internship experiences. "More than one-third (35%) of summer internships were cancelled due to the pandemic and another 24% were refashioned as virtual opportunities for students and recent graduates" (Adams, 2020, para 2). This wave lifted some of the barriers associated with in-person experiences giving organizations the freedom to explore innovative ways to conduct internships. Networking can be difficult in a virtual environment, but companies like Amazon took on the challenge by hosting weekly "fireside" chats via remote video conferencing to expand mentoring opportunities (Chan, 2020). Other companies held weekly virtual meetings with interns and staff, virtual worksite tours; virtual interviews with industry professionals; and virtual mentoring sessions (ACTE, 2020). Still many companies have used this pandemic to explore how they do "work" in general and continue to work to incorporate these new strategies into their workforce moving forward. Hering (2020) found that there was a 159% increase in remote work between 2005 and 2017. During the COVID-19 pandemic, 66% of U.S. employees worked remotely, at least part-time (Herhold, 2020). The pandemic emphasized how virtual internships bring value to education, and many institutions are beginning to recognize them as important forms of experiential learning in the development of student skills and competencies despite the circumstances that warrant their use.

Internships from a Theoretical Perspective

This book was, in part, designed to help the reader explore the role and structure, benefits and intended outcomes, and the challenges of internships in undergraduate business education. As we explore these areas, understanding the theories that guide practice can be helpful in our understanding of internships and how best to use them moving forward.

Constructivism is a theory that explains how learners create knowledge. It represents a wide range of perspectives while asserting that we "*construct*" our own meaning rather than meaning being discovered (Merriam, Caffarella, & Baumgartner, 2007). True meaning emerges when human consciousness engages with objects (Crotty, 1998). Constructivists also believe that meanings are both subjective and objective. Paul and Mukhopadhyay (2005) note that, unlike the positivist era that dealt primarily in scientific knowledge, constructivist take values into consideration. The constructivist perspective is evident in multiple theories of learning; however, I find the following most helpful in my analysis of internships: contextual teaching and learning, situated learning, work-based learning, and cognitive apprenticeships (Figure 2.1).

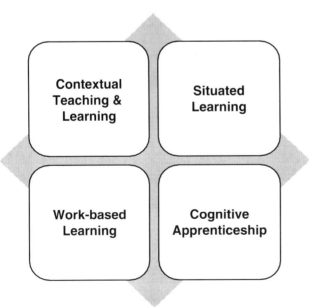

Figure 2.1 Constructivist Theories of Learning.

Contextual Teaching and Learning

Contextual teaching and learning (CTL) uses eight interrelated components to help students make meaning of and retain course material (Johnson, 2002). By using this process, students are able to determine the viewpoints that people seek while developing steps to give meaning to the context that has been discovered (Johnson, 2002). Johnson (2002) defined the process as follows:

> The CTL system is an educational process that aims to help students see meaning in the academic material they are studying by connecting academic subjects with the context of their daily lives, that is, with the context of their personal, social, and cultural circumstances. To achieve this aim, the system encompasses the following eight components: making meaningful connections, doing significant work, self-regulated learning, collaborating, critical and creative thinking, nurturing the individual, reaching high standards, and using authentic assessment.
> (Johnson, 2002, p. 25)

The eight components of contextual teaching and learning assisted in my understanding of how administrators and employers structure internships and my interpretation of the role they have in student development. When viewed through contextual teaching/learning, students are able to make meaning of their academic preparation by reflecting on the relationship between the internship and their course material. Internships involve an integration of the eight components of contextual teaching/learning. Therefore, a thorough understanding of this theory is helpful in understanding how students make meaning of course material, how they create new knowledge, and how practitioners and employers design internship experiences to meet the needs of all stakeholders involved.

Situated Learning

Situated learning is a "social-cultural process" (Zhang, Kaufman, Schell, Salgado, Seah, & Jeremic 2017, p. 3) centered around making gradual connections within communities that later lead to full participation (Lave & Wenger, 1991). Lave and Wenger (1991) posit that the connections we make within the community demonstrate how important our environment is in our ability to create new knowledge. They believe that learning is a naturally occurring action deeply rooted within activity, context, and culture (Lave & Wenger, 1991). Situated learning shifts the learning process from an individual focus to a participatory focus (Quay, 2003). "Of prime importance in situated learning is the conceptualization of the intimate connection between participation and the social and cultural world within which that participation occurs, a viewpoint often missed in many models of learning in experiential education" (Quay, 2003, p. 107). Situated learning theory provides an essential framework to analyze the structure of internships at companies that recruit business interns. It also provides insight into how employers engage interns in the social, cultural, and professional life of the organization.

During an internship, students make connections with mentors, supervisors, and potential colleagues. Employers make connections with potential employees and administrators make connections with industry professionals able to provide professional opportunities for the students they serve. The process is cyclical and as these connections are made, they continually demonstrate the value of situated learning by showing how important our communities are in our ability to create new knowledge.

Work-Based Learning

Work-based learning often refers to work that occurs in a place of business resulting from a need to resolve a workplace issue (Lester & Costley, 2010). It overlaps with experiential learning, but is not the same, and is frequently informal in nature (Lester & Costley, 2010). Much of the learning received in the workplace is outside the scope of what higher education institutions traditionally engage; however, when planned and organized it has the capacity to gain value through university involvement (Lester & Costley, 2010). When institutions and employers work together, work-based learning provides an opportunity to create a space for the development of new learning opportunities in the workplace (Boud, Solomon, & Symes, 2001; Roodhouse, 2010). To achieve this goal, institutions will often view work-based learning as a field of study receiving formal accreditation as a university course (Costley, 2001; Roodhouse, 2010). According to Boud, Solomon, and Symes (2001), work-based learning programs in higher education typically share the following six characteristics:

- A partnership between an external organization and an educational institution;
- Learners are actual employees of the organization;
- The work performed at the organization is the curriculum;
- Current competencies and desired learning outcomes are identified before the learner begins the process;
- Projects and assignments take place in the actual workplace; and
- Institutions assess the learning outcomes based on a pre-established framework accepted by both the institution and the employer.

Organizations that commit to work-based learning partnerships are typically larger and make a great investment of time and resources to ensure the development of its employees (Boud, Solomon, & Symes, 2001). This type of learning demonstrates a key example of how academia and industry work together to ensure that learners gain skills, credentials, and wages to help them succeed in the labor market (Rodriguez, Fox, & McCambly, 2016). Lester and Costley (2010) found a "growing body of evidence to indicate that work-based learning of various kinds is effective in increasing adult participation in higher education and in developing the capability of individuals and organizations" (p. 567). Therefore, work-based learning provides an ideal framework to analyze how schools and employers work together to overcome challenges and increase the benefits and intended outcomes of internships for both groups. When industry and education work together, new knowledge has a platform on which to emerge.

Cognitive Apprenticeship

The cognitive apprenticeship is a method of teaching the learner different ways of thinking about the activity they are involved and its associated skills (Brandt, Farmer, & Buckmaster, 1993; Merriam, Caffarella, & Baumgartner, 2007). According to Brandt, Farmer, and Buckmaster (1993), "cognitive apprenticeship is a vehicle for tapping the knowledge and experience of adults who have found ways to effectively handle the tasks, problems, and problematic situations in the current era" (p. 69). Cognitive apprenticeships are often demonstrated using a five-phase process: modeling, approximating, fading, self-directed learning, and generalizing (Brandt, Farmer, & Buckmaster, 1993). According to Brandt, Farmer, and Buckmaster (1993), the five phases include the following characteristics:

- Modeling: the learner observes a real-life activity in totality in order to verbally articulate the action;
- Approximating: requires the learner to perform the activity while receiving support and coaching from the instructor;
- Fading: the learner becomes more independent while feedback from the instructor is minimized;
- Self-directed learning: the instructor provides assistance only when asked and the learner takes the initiative to present the activity alone or in a group within a specified time frame deemed appropriate to the situation; and
- Generalizing: the instructor and learner discuss the new skill and the learner is then encouraged to use it in new situations.

According to Brandt, Farmer, and Buckmaster (1993), what makes cognitive apprenticeships so powerful is the focus on "learning how to learn" (p. 77), the interaction of the learner with a knowledgeable instructor, and the responsibility of the learner to verbally articulate their thoughts. The cognitive apprenticeship model demonstrates how important supervisors are in the learner's ability to understand and articulate new skills. Structured internships have the ability to provide a platform for students to engage in this five-phase approach to learning. Therefore, when executed correctly, it often produces knowledge that could not be realized in a traditional classroom setting.

Conclusion

Constructivist theories of learning are significant in understanding the role, structure, benefits, and intended outcomes of internships in postsecondary business education. By viewing internships in business through the lens' described, we are able to recognize the importance of creating meaning from concrete experiences and understand why a focus on the process of learning is central in our ability to positively affect the outcome of learning. When there is a better understanding of how learners create knowledge, business educators may have a better understanding of how internships can enhance the curricula, decrease the skills gap, and produce graduates that satisfy the needs of our growing labor market (Griffis, 2014; Tanyel, Mitchell, & McAlum, 1999).

Chapter Quiz
1. What has long been described as the process of "learning by doing"?
2. What is considered the preferred method of experiential learning for business schools worldwide to give students practical experiences and help them transition to the real world?
3. What are the active learning practices that promote deep learning by promoting student engagement?
4. Alon (2003) noted that several skills are developed as a result of experiential learning. Name the 4 skills mentioned.
5. Experiential learning typifies which three AACSB directives?

6. Name two popular alternatives to the traditional internships offered in many colleges and schools of business.
7. What serves as a visual representation of how "knowledge is created through the transformation of experience"?
8. Which perspective asserts that we "construct" our own meaning rather than meaning being discovered?
9. What is a "social-cultural process" centered around making gradual connections within communities that later lead to full participation?
10. What often refers to work that occurs in a place of business resulting from a need to resolve a workplace issue?

Quiz Answers:
1. Experiential learning
2. Internships
3. HIPs (High Impact Practices)
4. Communication, teamwork, problem-solving, and critical thinking
5. Innovation, impact, and engagement
6. International internships and virtual internships
7. David Kolb's experiential learning model
8. Constructivist
9. Situated learning
10. Work-based learning

References

ACT. (2017). *Understanding and solving the skills gap*. Retrieved from https://www.act.org/content/dam/act/unsecured/documents/understanding-and-solving-the-skills-gap.pdf

Adams, R. D. (2020). *Quarantine class of 2020: Virtual internships surge during coronavirus pandemic*. Retrieved from https://www.techrepublic.com/article/quarantine-class-of-2020-virtual-internships-surge-during-coronavirus-pandemic/

Alon, I. (2003). Experiential learning in international business via the worldwide web. *The Journal of Teaching in International Business*, *14*(2), 79–98.

Association to Advance Collegiate Schools of Business. (2018). *Business standards*. Retrieved from https://www.aacsb.edu/accreditation/standards/business#gsc.tab=0

Association to Advance Collegiate Schools of Business. (2016). *Accreditation standards*. Retrieved from http://www.aacsb.edu/accreditation/standards

Association for Career & Technical Education. (2020). High-quality CTE: Planning for a COVID-19 impacted school year. Retrieved from https://www.acteonline.org/wp-content/uploads/2020/06/Planning_for_COVID-19-impacted_Year_FINAL.pdf

Beard, D., Schwieger, D., & Surendran, K. (2008). Integrating soft skills assessment through university, college, and programmatic efforts at an AACSB accredited institution. *Journal of Information Systems Education*, *19*(2), 229–240.

Bennis, W. G. & O'Toole, J. (2005). How business schools lost their way. *Harvard Business Review*, *83*(5), 96–104, 154.

Birch, C., Allen, J., McDonald, J., & Tomaszczyk, E. (2010). Graduate Internships-bridging the academic and vocational divide. In S. Halley, C. Birch, D. T. Tempelaar, M. McCuddy, N. Hernàndez Nanclares, S. Reeb-Gruber, W. H. Gijselaers, B. Rienties, & E. Nelissen (Eds.), *Proceedings of the 17th EDINEB Conference: Crossing borders in education and work-based learning* (pp. 194–195). London: FEBA ERD Press.

Boud, D., Solomon, N., & Symes, C. (2001). New practices for new times. In D. Boud & N. Solomon (Eds.), *Work-based learning: A new higher education?* (pp. 18–33). Buckingham: Open University Press & Society for Research into Higher Education.

Brandt, B. L., Farmer, J. A., & Buckmaster, A. (1993). Cognitive apprenticeship approach to helping adults learn. *New Directions for Adults and Continuing Education, 59*, 69–78. DOI: 10.1002/ace.36719935909

Caulfield, J., & Woods, T. (2013). Experiential learning: Exploring its long-term impact on socially responsible behavior. *Journal of the Scholarship of Teaching and Learning, 13*(2), 31–48.

Chan, K. (2020). *Internships get canceled or go virtual because of pandemic*. Retrieved from https://www.pbs.org/newshour/nation/internships-get-canceled-or-go-virtual-because-of-pandemic

Coco, M. (2000). Internships: A try before you buy arrangement. *SAM Advanced Management Journal, 65*(2), 41–47.

Costley, C. (2001). Organizational and employee interest in programs of work-based learning. *Learning Organization, 8*(2), 58–63.

Crotty, M. (1998). *The foundations of social research*. London: SAGE Publications.

Divine, R. L., Linrud, J. K., Miller, R. H., & Wilson, J. H. (2007). Required internship programs in marketing: Benefits, challenges, and determinants of fit. *Marketing Education Review, 17*, 45–52.

Eisner, S. (1999). The impact of business school on student attitudes towards diversity in the 21st century workplace. *Transformations, 10*(1), 49. Retrieved from https://login.proxy.lib.fsu.edu/login?url=http://search.proquest.com/docview/220383150?accountid=4840

Eyler, J., & Giles, D. E. (1999). *Whereas the learning in service-learning?* San Francisco: Jossey-Bass.

Fenwick, T. J. (2000). Expanding conceptions of experiential learning: A review of the five contemporary perspectives on cognition. *Adult Education Quarterly, 50*(4), 243.

Fenwick, T. J. (2001). Experiential learning: A theoretical critique from five perspectives. Columbus, OH: Centre on Education and Training for Employment.

Fenwick, T. J. (2003). Learning through experience: Troubling orthodoxies and intersecting questions.Malabar, FL: Krieger Publishing Company.

Gault, J., Leach, E., & Duey, M. (2010). Effects of business internships on job marketability: the employers' perspective. *Education + Training, 1*(*52*), 76–88.

Gault, J., Redington, J., & Schlager, T. (2000). Undergraduate business internships and career success: Are they related? *Journal of Marketing Education, 22*, 45–53.

Gerken, M., Rienties, B., Giesbers, B., & Konings, K. D. (2012). Enhancing the academic internship learning experience for business education – A critical review and future directions. In P. G. C. Van den Bossche, W. H. Gijselaers, R. G. Milter (Eds.), *Learning at the Crossroads of Theory and Practice (pp.)*. Heidelberg: Springer. doi: 10.1007/978-94-007-2846-2_1

Grair, C. A. (2007). Experiential learning in business German workshops. *Global Business Languages, 7*(8), 1–21. Retrieved from http://docs.lib.purdue.edu/gbl/vol7/iss1/8

Govekar, M. A., & Rishi, M. (2007). Service learning: Bringing real-world education into the B-school classroom. *Journal of Education for Business, 83*(1), 3–10.

Griffis, P. J. (2014). Information literacy in business education experiential learning programs. *Journal of Business & Finance Librarianship, 19*, 333–341. DOI: 10.1080/08963568.2014.952987

Hager, P. (2011). Theories of workplace learning. In Malloch, Cairns, Evans, & O'Connor (Eds.), *The sage handbook of workplace learning (pp. 17–31)*. London: SAGE Publications.

2008 Hart Research Associates. (2008). *How should colleges assess and improve student learning? Employers views on the accountability challenge*. Washington, DC: Association of American Colleges and Universities.

Hergert, M. (2009). Student perceptions of the value of internships in business education. *American Journal of Business Education, 2*(8), 9–13.

Herhold, K. (2020). *66% of U.S. employees are working remotely at least part-time during the COVID-19 pandemic*. Retrieved from https://www.prnewswire.com/news-releases/66-of-us-employees-are-working-remotely-at-least-part-time-during-the-covid-19-pandemic-301041859.html

Hering, B. B. (2020). *Remote work statistics: Shifting norms and expectations*. Retrieved from https://www.flexjobs.com/blog/post/remote-work-statistics/

Hiltebeitel, K. M., Leauby, B. A., & Larkin, J. M. (2000). Job satisfaction among entry-level accountants. *CPA Journal, 5*(70), 76–79.

Hodge, L., Proudford, K. L., & Holt, H. (2014). From periphery to core: The increasing relevance of experiential learning in undergraduate business education. *Research in Higher Education Journal, 26*, 1–17.

Hurst, J. L., & Good, L. K. (2010). A 20-year evolution of internships: Implications for retail interns, employers and educators. *The International Review of Retail, Distribution and Consumer Research, 20*(1), 175–186. doi: http://dx.doi.org/10.1080/09593960903498342

Johnson, E. B. (2002). *Contextual teaching and learning: What it is and why it's here to stay*. Thousand Oaks, CA: Corwin Press.

Kavas, A. (2013). Skills needed for a global economy: Challenges and opportunities for rebuilding business curriculum. *Journal of International Finance & Economics, 13*(1), 29–34.

Kolb, A. Y., & Kolb, D. A. (2008). Experiential learning theory: A dynamic, holistic approach to management learning, education and development. In Armstrong & Fukami (Eds.), *The SAGE handbook of management learning, education, and development* (pp. 42–68. London: SAGE publications.

Kolb, A. Y., & Kolb, D. A. (2009). The learning way: Meta-cognitive aspects of experiential learning [Special Issue.]. *Simulation & Gaming, 40*(3), 297–327. Retrieved from https:doi.org/10.1177/1046878108325713

Kolb, D. A. (2015). *Experiential learning: Experience as the source of learning and development* (2nd Edition). Hoboken, NJ: Pearson Education.

Kolb, A. Y., & Kolb, D. A. (2017). Experiential learning theory as a guide for experiential educators in higher education. *Experiential Learning & Teaching in Higher Education: A Journal for Engaged Educators, 1*(1), 7–44. Retrieved from https://learningfromexperience.com/downloads/research-library/experiential-learning-theory-guide-for-higher-education-educators.pdf

Knemeyer, A. M., & Murphy, P. R. (2002). Logistics internships employer and student perspectives. *International Journal of Physical Distribution & Logistics Management, 2*(32), 135–152.

Knouse, S. B. & Fontenot, G. (2008). Benefits of the business college internship: a research review. *Journal of employment counseling, 45*(2), 61–66.

Kosnik, R. D., Tingle, J. K., & Blanton, E. L. (2013). Transformational learning in business education: The pivotal role of experiential learning projects. *American Journal of Business Education, 6*(6), 615–630.

Kumar, S. & Bhandarker, A. (2017). Experiential learning and its relevance in business school curriculum. *Developments in Business Simulation and Experiential Learning, 44*, 244–251.

Kuh, G. D. & O'Donnell, K. (2013). *Ensuring quality and taking high-impact practices to scale*. Washington, DC: Association of American Colleges and Universities.

Kuh, G. D. & Schneider, C. G. (2008). *High-impact educational practices: what they are, who has access to them, and why they matter*. Washington, DC: Association of American Colleges and Universities.

Lave, J. & Wenger, E. (1991). *Situated learning: Legitimate peripheral participation*. Cambridge: Cambridge University Press.

Lester, S. & Costley, C. (2010). Work-based learning at higher education level: value, practice and critique. *Studies in Higher Education, 35*(5), 561–575.

Lord, D. R., Sumrall, D. & Sambandam, R. (2011). Satisfaction determinants in business internships. *Interdisciplinary Journal of Contemporary Research in Business, 10*(2), 11–22.

McCarthy, P. R., & McCarthy, H. M. (2006). When case studies are not enough: Integrating experiential learning into business curricula. *Journal of Education for Business, 81*(4), 201–204.

McLeod, S. (2017). *Kolb's learning styles and experiential learning cycle*. Retrieved from https://www.simplypsychology.org/learning-kolb.html

Merriam, S. B., Caffarella, R. S., & Baumgartner, L. M. (2007). *Learning in adulthood: A comprehensive guide*. San Francisco: Jossey Bass.

Miettinen, R. (2000). The concept of experiential learning and John Dewey's theory of reflective thought and action. *International Journal of Lifelong Education, 19*(1), 54–72.

Moghaddam, J. M. (2011). Perceived effectiveness of business internships: student expectations, experiences and personality traits. *International Journal of Management*, 4(*28*), 287–303.

Moore, C., Barry, L. B., & Dooley, K. E. (2010). The effects of experiential learning with an emphasis on reflective writing on deep-level processing of leadership students. *Journal of Leadership in Education*, 9(1), 36–52.

Paul, P., & Mukhopadhyay, K. (2005). Experiential learning in international business education. *Journal of Teaching in International Business*, 16(2), 7–25.

Quay, J. (2003). Experience and participation: Relating theories of learning. *The Journal of Experiential Education*, 26(2), 105–116.

Rizk, L. (2011, May). *Learning by doing: Toward an experiential approach to professional development*. Paper presented at the meeting of the International Federation of Library Associations and Institutions, Puerto Rico.

Rodriguez, J., Fox, H., & McCambly, H. (2016). *Work-based learning as a pathway to postsecondary and career success* (Issue Brief No. 18). Retrieved from Illinois University Office of Community College Research and Leadership website: https://occrl.illinois.edu/docs/librariesProvider4/ptr/wbl-brief.pdf.

Rothman, M. (2007). Business students' evaluation of their internships. *Psychological Reports*, 1(*101*), 319–322.

Rothman, M., & Sisman, R. (2016). Internship impact on career consideration among business students. *Education + Training*, 58(9), 1003–1013.

Roodhouse, S. (2010). Defining and theorizing university work-based learning. In J. Mumford & S. Roodhouse (Eds.), *Understanding work-based learning* (pp. 21–28). New York: Routledge.

Rosenstein, A., Sweeney, C., & Gupta, R. (2012). Cross-disciplinary faculty perspectives on experiential learning. *Contemporary Issues in Education Research*. 5(3).

Ruggiero, D., & Boehm, J. (2016). Design and development of a learning design virtual internship program. *International Review of Research in Open and Distributed Learning*, 17(4), 105–120.

Smith, R. (2015, June). *College doesn't prepare students for full-time jobs-internships do. Fortune Insider*. Retrieved from http://fortune.com/2015/06/16/ryan-smith-internship-advice/

Sciglimpaglia, D., & Toole, H. R. (2009). Use of student field-based consulting in business education: A comparison of American and Australian business schools. *Journal of Education for Business*, 85(2), 68-77.

Silberman, M. (Ed.). (2007). *The handbook of experiential learning*. San Francisco: John Wiley & Sons, Inc.

Tanyel, F., Mitchell, M. A., & McAlum, H. G. (1999). The skill set for success of new business school graduates: Do prospective employers and university faculty agree? *Journal of Education for Business*, 79(1), 33–37.

Templeton, W., Updyke, K., & Bennett, R. B. (2012). Internships and the assessment of student learning. *Business Education & Accreditation*, 4(2), 27–38. 39

University of Colorado Denver. (2015). *Experiential learning center*. Retrieved from http://www.ucdenver.edu/life/services/ExperientialLearning/about/Pages/WhatisExperientialLearning.aspx

University of Texas at Austin. (2016). *Experiential learning defined: What is experiential learning*. Retrieved from https://facultyinnovate.utexas.edu/teaching/engagement/experiential-learning/defined

University Wisconsin Eau Claire. (2020). *High-impact practices*. Retrieved from https://www.uwec.edu/acadaff/academic-master-plan/high-impact-practices/

Vriens, M. (2015). Virtual internships: what's in it for business schools? *European Forum for Management Development Business Magazine*, 9(3), 62–65.

Zhang, F., Kaufman, D., Schell, R., Salgado, G, Seah, E. T. W., & Jeremic, J. (2017). Situated learning through intergenerational play between older adults and undergraduates. *International Journal of Educational Technology in Higher Education*, 14(16), 1–16. Doi: 10.1186/s41239-017-0055-0

Zhang, X. (2012). Discussion on international internship and intercultural competence from a perspective of higher educational internationalization – A case study of the program work and travel USA. *Cross-Cultural Communication*, 8(5), 62–66.

3 The Skills Gap

"Excellence is not a gift, but a skill that takes practice."

Plato

Skills Gap Defined

After going blind at the age 14, Erik Weihenmayer went on to became the first blind person to reach the summit of Mount Everest. Erik may not be a household name, but his accomplishments are certainly noteworthy. This adventurer, speaker, author, and former teacher knows what it means to have confidence and skill. Unfortunately, students are entering the workforce with increased confidence in their abilities while employer's expectations remain unmet (Stewart, Wall, & Marciniec, 2016). Oftentimes, we think of gaps as holes or breaks in something, but when we change our mindset, we see a golden opportunity to fill those gaps with skills that set us apart and make us more marketable. We are all gifted with skills and talents that set us apart from each other. When those skills come together, we can all accomplish more.

A growing number of industry professionals are expressing concern about the skill level of their new hires and the increasing skills gap that exists among recent college graduates (Cappelli, 2015). When the skills of the employee do not match the skills needed by the employer, a disconnect occurs that negatively effects the employee/manager relationship and the effective execution of assigned tasks. According to Cappelli (2015), the skills gap is often attributed to a failure in the public education system. Unfortunately, many young adults are entering the workforce with technical aptitude (or hard skills) and basic job knowledge, but lack the soft skills necessary to obtain and maintain quality employment (Beard, Schwieger, & Surendran, 2008; Blaszczynski & Green, 2012; Tulgan, 2015). Blaszczynski 2012 Tulgan 2015 Soft skills have been defined as a combination of interpersonal and social skills that include areas such as communication, collaboration, problem-solving, listening, flexibility, and humbleness (Blaszczynski & Green, 2012; Tulgan, 2015). These "non-technical competencies associated with one's personality, attitude, and ability to interact effectively with others" contribute significantly to an individual's job success (Stewart, Wall, & Marciniec, 2016, p. 276). A survey conducted by the *Wall Street Journal* found that 92% of executives see "soft skills as equally important or more important than technical skills" (Davidson, 2016, para. 11). "[Eighty-nine percent] of those same respondents emphasized that they have a hard time finding employees that possess these traits irrespective of age and experience level" (Davidson, 2016, para. 11). Business leaders and managers are concerned that new job candidates have not learned basic skills at home, high school, or even college (Tulgan, 2015). Tulgan (2015) noted that most managers feel that it should not be their responsibility to address the skills gap in new employees citing a lack of time, ability, and resources as primary reasons. Instead, these skills should be learned prior to entering the workforce; yet, many organizations are left to handle these deficiencies which cost them a significant amount of time and money (Tulgan, 2015).

Research on skill development can be traced back to the 1970s with the work of Professor Ivar Berg who asserted that early training on skill development was not effective but was developed with intentions other than enhancing individual employability skills (Cappelli, 2015). This study was the catalyst for increased research on skill development and skill mismatch in the years following; however, the majority of this research occurred outside of the United States (Cappelli, 2015). Stephen Vaisey's study of the mismatch between education and occupation in America is perhaps the most direct representation of research on skill development in the United States (Cappelli, 2015). Vaisey (2006) concluded that a large number of Americans are skilled, but those skills are beyond what is needed for the positions they occupy, causing an increased number of overqualified individuals to inhabit the workspace; a disparity that will continue to grow.

According to Cappelli (2015), most data on skill development has been obtained from job assessments and employer/employee feedback; therefore, research is limited and often presents contradictory information. In addition, "education levels are much easier to assess than skill levels" (Cappelli, 2015, p. 266). Nevertheless, skills have been widely viewed as the largest area of job growth (Cappelli, 2015) and employers continue to seek ways to develop employees with the skills they need for job success.

Generational Impact

The soft skills gap is widening from one generation to the next with Generation Z representing a "tipping point in the post-Boomer generational shift transforming the workforce" (Tulgan, 2018, para 6; Tulgan, 2015, p. 12). Generation Z consists of individuals born between 1995 and 2010 (Iorgulescu, 2016; Seemiller & Grace, 2015). What makes this generation unique are the historical events that have occurred since their birth (Seemiller & Grace, 2015; Tulgan, 2015). Globalization, technology, institutional uncertainty, the information environment, and human diversity have all played a significant role in this generation's beliefs and attitudes toward work (Tulgan, 2015).

Generation Z is more familiar with working across borders; multi-tasking; adjusting to changing technologies and uncertainties about the economy; accessing information electronically; communicating using multiple digital devices; and working with various cultures in what many believe to be the most diverse workforce in history (Iorgulescu, 2016; Seemiller & Grace, 2015; Tulgan, 2015). While these changes present amazing opportunities for workforce development, they also present conflicting ideas between generations on how work should be performed (Seemiller & Grace, 2015). By gaining a better understanding of the generations in the workforce, we gain greater insight into why the skills gap is widening and how identification of the issues can help address concerns.

Baby Boomers, the generation born between 1946 and 1964, grew up with traditional values that included an 8-to-5 work schedule, a strong appreciation for hard work, and a belief in the importance of work-life balance (Fogg, 2009; Mencl & Lester, 2014;

Seemiller & Grace, 2015). They grew up in an era where positivity and opportunity were instilled in them from birth (Zemke, Filipczak, & Raines, 2013). In contrast, Generation X, born between 1965 and 1980, grew up at the height of cable television and the growing trend of having both parents working outside of the home, which gave them a sense of independence (Seemiller & Grace, 2015). However, they still managed to treasure the work-life balance principle that their parents so diligently sought to maintain (Cennamo & Gardner, 2008; Glass, 2007; Seemiller & Grace, 2015).

Generation Y, also known as Millennials and sometimes referred to as the "*me-generation,*" exude a sense of entitlement, have high career expectations, are consumed by technology, and have close relationships with parents (DelCampo, Haggerty, & Knippel, 2011; Mencl & Lester, 2014; Seemiller & Grace, 2015). A study conducted by Twenge and Foster (2010) found that students classified as Generation Y in 2006 were 30% more narcissistic than their counterparts in 1982. This *self-involved* focus played a significant role in workplace behavior and relationships. Millennials are also viewed as highly educated and tolerant of cultural differences, but strongly oppose the traditional 8-to-5 workday to which previous generations are accustomed (DelCampo, Haggerty, & Knippel, 2011; Seemiller & Grace, 2015).

The generations differ in various ways, but they also share similarities that transcend age. A study conducted by Lester, Standifer, Schultz, and Windsor (2012) found that while generations placed a different value on teamwork and collaboration, all viewed these characteristics as important and desire to engage in collaborative work at some level in their professions. In addition, Baby Boomers and Generation Y both value flexibility in work in order to maintain a work-life balance that helps Baby Boomers, in particular, with personal demands such as taking care of elderly parents (Hill, Hawkins, Ferris, & Weitzman, 2001; Hewlett, Sherbin, & Sumberg 2009).

According to Tulgan (2015), Generation Z is accustomed to making their own rules and only conforming to the directives of a parent or guardian; therefore, they find it difficult to understand how "old-fashioned" soft skills could benefit an employer, let alone themselves. As Millennials enter the workforce and Generation Z matriculates through college, employers increasingly recognize that "you can't hire your way around the soft skills gap" (Tulgan, 2015, p. 33). No matter how highly trained an employee may be in the hard skills, all new employees require some type of onboarding and on-the-job training that should include some component of soft skills training that strategically informs the new hire of the policies and practices of their new employer (Tulgan, 2015). Continued research on the generations provides a significant resource to educate employers and "eliminate unfounded generational stereotypes" (Mencl & Lester, 2014, p. 269). This knowledge can aid in the creation of a more collaborative work environment that embraces the diversity that each generation brings to the workforce.

Skills for the Future

Increases in technology and other alternative ways of work have revolutionized the workforce by increasing productivity and our ability to do more with less. However, these innovations have not diminished the need for skills that go beyond the intellectual, hands-on abilities that often receive so much attention. Soft skills, personal characteristics that aid in our ability to work well with others, are crucial in today's labor market. Yet, employers continue to express concern over the lack of soft skills they find in recent hires. The National Association of Colleges and Employers (2015) identified the following as the top 10 soft skills that employers seek in college graduates: leadership, teamwork, written communication, problem-solving, verbal communication, work ethic, initiative, analytical/quantitative skills, flexibility/adaptability, and staying current on changing technologies.

According to Laker and Powell (2011), research on soft skills and hard skills training is scarce. The latter may be due to the belief that hard skills training has been guided by practice and not theory (Swanson & Holton, 1997; Williams, 2001). In 2015, the Society of Human Resource Management conducted a study to determine employer perception of the skills their new employee's lack. Those skills included professionalism/work ethic; relationship building; business acumen; written communications; critical thinking/problem-solving; leadership; lifelong learning/self-direction; teamwork/collaboration; coaching skills; and flexibility/openness to new experiences (Stewart, Wall, & Marciniec, 2016). Both studies demonstrate the important role that soft skills play in professional success; however, concern continues to grow as employers work to identify candidates that meet their employment needs in both the hard and soft areas of skill development.

Most soft skills are learned through active participation in activities that occur outside of a textbook or a traditional classroom lecture (Blaszczynski & Green, 2012; Halsey, 2011; Stewart, Wall, & Marciniec, 2016). According to Stewart, Wall, and Marciniec (2016), some organizations have introduced soft skill development training into the workplace; however, those programs are typically the first to be cut from the budget because of the difficulty in measuring return on investment. Halsey (2011) suggests that the 70/30 principle could help educators shift their focus to include more active learning in the teaching environment. In this approach, learners do 70% of the talking and 30% of the listening; educators spend 70% of their time designing the learning experience and 30% determining the content to be taught; and learners spend 30% of the time learning (e.g., being taught) and 70% of the time practicing what they've learned (Halsey, 2011). While this suggestion deviates from the common practices found among faculty in postsecondary business education, the emphasis on active student learning could reap benefits for students, employers, and institutions alike.

Faculty play a primary role in curriculum reform. In 1966, the American Association of University Professors (AAUP) declared their position on faculty involvement in curriculum reform by updating its position statement, designating faculty as responsible for "curriculum, methods of instruction, research and faculty status, among other factors" (Duffy, 2015; p. 12). In 1987, the National Education Association (1987) also affirmed that faculty members have primary responsibility for developing course content that addresses the needs of a diverse student population; therefore, reform efforts cannot "succeed without adequate support for the faculty" (p. 9). While the faculty role remains clear, it also partially explains why curriculum changes that address the skills gap are sometimes difficult to implement in higher education. According to Tanyel, Mitchell, and McAlum (1999), politics and conflicting thoughts among faculty about what constitutes a legitimate and worthwhile curriculum change often necessitates a slow response to reform initiatives. Regardless of the reformation process, research continues to show that mastering soft skills is just as essential as the development of hard skills (Blaszczynski & Green, 2012; Dixon, Belnmap, Albrecht, & Lee, 2010; Wilhelm, 2002). With this knowledge, it becomes imperative that postsecondary business education take a closer look at ways to address these mounting concerns in order to produce graduates with the skills employers need.

Leadership Skills in Business

Nelson and Quick (1995) defined leadership as "the process of guiding and directing the behavior of people in the work environment" (p. 358). While this definition is still applicable, leadership has undergone an evolution in formal characterization, but the premise remains the same. Leadership is often noted as one of the top skills that employers seek in new hires; yet, many students are entering the workforce lacking this proficiency (National Association of Colleges and Employers, 2015; Stewart, Wall, & Marciniec, 2016). Courses on leadership development are common in the undergraduate business curriculum, but are not required by all business programs (Colby, Ehrilich, Sullivan, & Dolle, 2011). Programs that teach leadership often do so through an organizational behavior course (Nirenberg, 1998). According to Nirenberg (1998), these courses need to be re-evaluated to ensure that students are learning the realities of leadership and not the myths.

No longer can individuals assume that a person in a leadership role is equipped with the skills necessary to effectively guide the thoughts and actions of others. Nirenberg (1998) found that leadership is a process that requires the leader to gain respect from subordinates. According to Nichols and Cottrell (2014), good leaders are trustworthy and competent. They give the subordinate confidence in knowing that a goal can be reached without the leader taking advantage of them or the situation (Nichols & Cottrell, 2014).

According to Pfeffer (2009), "business schools see themselves as being in the business of producing leaders for both public and private sector organizations" (p. 2). However, when companies feel that employee skills do not match the skills they need, many take the initiative to create their own programs to help fill the gap. Leadership development programs, internal universities, and partnerships with leadership professionals are some of the approaches that companies have taken to improve employee leadership development (Pfeffer, 2009). A survey conducted in 2001 found that the most successful companies in the development of strong leaders are those that provide adequate resources and programs, along with sufficient time for senior management to get involved in leadership development activities (Pfeffer, 2009).

Leadership development has become a profitable business for business schools and companies alike through the creation of leadership development centers, endowed chairs in leadership, and the billions of dollars that companies spend each year to offer leadership training to its employees (Gomez, 2007; Pfeffer, 2009). Nirenberg (1998) found that "leadership is not a function of the position, but a role that everyone can (and will) play" (p. 94). Therefore, it becomes imperative that preparing students with leadership skills remain a priority as the undergraduate business curriculum is developed and enhanced.

A report released by the Organization for Economic Co-operation and Development (Organization for Economic Co-operation and Development, 2018), found that by the year 2030, the following types of skills will be necessary for success in the workforce: (a) cognitive and meta-cognitive skills, (b) social and emotional skills, and (c) practical and physical skills. Cognitive and meta-cognitive skills include critical thinking, creative thinking, learning-to-learn, and self-regulation (Organization for Economic Co-operation and Development, 2018). "Cognitive skills are the core skills our brains use to think, read, learn, remember, reason, and pay attention" (Learning RX, 2020, para. 1). Social and emotional skills include empathy, self-efficacy, responsibility, and collaboration (Organization for Economic Co-operation and Development, 2018). They involve our

26   *The Skills Gap*

capacity to "cultivate relationships at home, school, work, and in the community, and exercise our civic responsibilities" (Organization for Economic Co-operation and Development, 2018, p. 4). This skill is often referred to as emotional intelligence. Practical and physical skills involve using new information and communication technology devices (Organization for Economic Co-operation and Development, 2018). For example, operating a tool requires the physical ability and the practical skill to use and manipulate the tool to achieve a specific outcome (Organization for Economic Co-operation and Development, 2018). Other examples of practical and physical skills include using technological devices, operating new machines, playing a musical instrument, and even life skills like preparing food and getting dressed (Organization for Economic Co-operation and Development, 2018).

We often see these types of skills manifested in terms like *critical thinking, teamwork, problem solving, self-control, emotional intelligence, communication, leadership,* and *technological competence*. Employers want skilled employees and employees need skills to thrive. Therefore, internships provide an ideal opportunity for the needs of both stakeholders to be met.

Increases in technology and other alternative ways of work have revolutionized the workforce by increasing productivity and our ability to do more with less. However, these innovations have not diminished the need for skills that go beyond the intellectual, hands-on abilities that often receive so much more attention.

What Can Students Do?

Everyone is gifted with skills. It is our responsibility to identify those skills and do the work to cultivate them. Internships provide an excellent opportunity for skill development, but internships are not the only opportunity to hone in on existing skills while developing new skills.

1. **Visit Your Career Center**
   Meet with a career services professional and take advantage of the career resources available in your career center. This can be an invaluable tool for skill development. It can include an individual career advising session, taking a career assessment, attending a career development workshop, or reviewing career resource material in the career library. The possibilities are endless, but the first step is to visit so that a career professional can provide guidance on your path to success.
2. **Take a Course**
   In addition to required courses, seek out elective courses that provide opportunity for you to discover a new skill or advance an existing skill. Examples include professional development, business communication, career development, public speaking, leadership development, and any other specialized course that your institution may provide. If you are unable to find a course on campus that meets your professional development needs, consider online options that you can complete at your own pace. For example, LinkedIn Learning, formerly known as Lydna.com, provides access to over 15,000 expert-led courses. Before purchasing access, check with your school to find out if access is already available through your institution.
3. **Volunteer**
   Volunteering not only helps you help others, but it can also help you expand your network, learn new skills, and advance your career. Volunteers can use those skills for the greater good of the community they serve.

4. **Join a Club**

    As you cultivate new relationships by joining a club, you also build social and emotional skills like empathy, self-efficacy, responsibility, and collaboration. According to the Organization for Economic Cooperation and Development (2018), by the year 2030, social and emotional skills will be one of three necessary skillsets to have for success in the workforce.

Practical Exercises

Exercise 1 – Identify and Execute

Purpose: To identify existing skills and develop strategies to improve your skillset

Activity: Review the following types of skills that were identified by the Organization for Economic Cooperation and Development (OECD) as necessary for success in the workforce by 2030:

- Cognitive and meta-cognitive skills
- Social and emotional skills
- Practical and physical skills

Use the chart below (Table 3.1) to complete the following tasks:

- In column 2, identify at least one skill in each category that you feel confident in your ability to effectively demonstrate.
- In column 3, describe how you have demonstrated that skill in your academic or professional life (e.g., internship, group project, part-time job, etc.).
- In column 4, list one skill from each category that you need to improve.
- In column 5, describe at least one plan of action that you will take to improve upon that skill.

An example is provided below in row 1.

Don't overthink this exercise. Take about 10 minutes. If an area of success requires too much thought, then it probably needs to be an area of improvement. The **goal** is to identify areas where you are strong and develop a plan of action for areas where you might be weak. By implementing strategies now, you make yourself more marketable moving forward.

Table 3.1 Identify and Execute

Skills Category	Area of Success	How skill is/was demonstrated	Area of improvement	Plan of action for improvement
Cognitive and meta-cognitive skills	ex. Creative Thinking	Developed a successful social media page for my internship employer	Critical Thinking	Read at least one new book per month
Social and emotional skills				
Practical and physical skills				

Exercise 2 – Skills Analysis

Use the chart below (Table 3.2) to complete the following assignment.

1. Locate a position description that interest you (e.g., internship, part-time job, or full-time job).
2. Identify the skills required for that position (e.g., skills valued by the company, skills required to do the job).
3. Circle the skills that you currently have.
4. Underline the skills that you need to develop.
5. Develop a plan of action to help you further develop those skills (e.g., university resources, online resources, people, classes, etc.).

Table 3.2 Skills Analysis

Position Title	
Required skills	•
	•
	•
	•
	•
	•
	•
Plan of Action	•
	•
	•
	•
	•
	•

Conclusion

During a series of interviews to fill an available position, I had a very difficult decision to make. The pool of applicants had been narrowed to two and both had a comparable educational background and work history. References were glowing and their ability to do the job well became more obvious with every conversation and reference check. But what took center stage was their social and emotional skills. Something as simple as a warm personality and sending a "thank-you" note can play a major role in our final decision-making process. While all skills are important, don't underestimate the power of the social skills (or soft skills). Teaching people the technical/hard skills is much easier than teaching the soft skills so when I'm forced to choose between the two, I often choose the latter.

References

Beard, D., Schwieger, D., & Surendran, K. (2008). Integrating soft skills assessment through university, college, and programmatic efforts at an AACSB accredited institution. *Journal of Information Systems Education, 19*(2), 229–240.

Blaszczynski, C., & Green, D. J. (2012). Effective strategies and activities for developing soft skill, part 1. *Journal of Applied Research for Business Instruction, 10*(1), 1–13.

Cappelli, P. H. (2015). Skills gaps, skill shortages, and skill mismatches: Evidence and arguments for the United States. *ILR Review, 68*(2), 25–290.

Cennamo, L., & Gardner, D. (2008). Generational differences in work values, outcomes and person-organization values fit. *Journal of Managerial Psychology, 23*, 891–906.

Colby, A., Ehrlich, T, Sullivan, W. M., & Dolle, J. R. (2011). *Rethinking undergraduate business education: Liberal learning for the profession.* San Francisco: Jossey-Bass.

Davison, K. (2016). Employers find 'soft skills' like critical thinking in short supply. *The Wall Street Journal,* Retrieved from https://www.wsj.com/articles/employers-find-soft-skills-like-critical-thinking-in-short-supply-1472549400.

DelCampo, R. G., Haggerty, L. A., & Knippel, L. A. (2011). *Managing the mulit-genrational workforce: From the GO Generation to the Millennials.* Abingdon: Routledge.

Dixon, J., Belnap, C, Albrech, C., & Lee, K. (2010). The importance of soft skills. *Corporate Finance Review, 14*(6), 35–38.

Duffy, C. (2015). *Leadership in business education curriculum reform: Faculty experiences responding to the skill gap crisis with special consideration of nontraditional students.* (Doctoral dissertation). California Lutheran University: Thousand Oaks, CA.

Fogg, P. (2009). When generations collide. *Education Digest, 74*, 25–30.

Glass, A. (2007). Understanding generational differences for competitive success. *Industrial and Commercial Training, 39*, 98–103.

Gomez, D. (2007, Spring). The leader as learner. *International Journal of Leadership Studies, 2*(3), 280–284.

Halsey, V. (2011). *Brilliance by design: Creating learning experiences that connect, inspire, and ENGAGE.* San Francisco: Berrett-Koehler Publishers.

Hewlett, S. A., Sherbin, L., & Sumberg, K. (2009). How Gen Y & Boomers will reshape your agenda. *Harvard Business Review, 87*(7-8), 71–76.

Hill, E. J., Hawkins, A. J., Ferris, M., & Weitzman, M. (2001). Finding an extra day a week: The positive influence of perceived job flexibility on work and family life balance. *Family Relations, 50,* 49–58.

Iorgulescu, M. C. (2016). Generation Z and its perception of work. *Cross-Cultural Management Journal, 1*(9), 47–54.

Laker, D. R., & Powell, J. (2011). The differences between hard and soft skills and their relative impact on training transfer. *Human Resource Development Quarterly, 22*(1), 111–122.

Learning, R. X. (2020). *What are cognitive skills?* Retrieved from https://www.learningrx.com/what-is-brain-training-/what-are-cognitive-skills-/

Lester, S. W., Standifer, R. L., Schultz, N. J., & Windsor, J. M. (2012). Actual versus perceived generational differences at work: An empirical examination. *Journal of Leadership & Organizational Studies, 19,* 341–354.

Mencl, J., & Lester, S. W. (2014). More alike than different: What generations value and how the values affect employee workplace perceptions. *Journal of Leadership & Organizational Studies, 21*(3), 257–272.

Metacognitive Skills. (2020). *What are metacognitive skills.* Retrieved from http://www.talenteducation.eu/toolkitforteachers/metacognicalskills/what-are-metacognitive-skills/

National Association of Colleges and Employers. (2015). *Job outlook 2016.* Bethlehem, PA.

National Education Association. (1987). Curriculum reform in higher education. Retrieved from http://files.eric.ed.gov/fulltext/ED309733.pdf

Nelson, D., & Quick, J. (1995). *Organizational behavior: Foundations, realities and challenges*. Minneapolis/St. Paul, MN: South-Western.

Nichols, A. L., & Cottrell, C. A. (2014). What do people desire in their leaders? The role of leadership level on trait desirability. *The Leadership Quarterly*, 25, 711–729.

Nirenberg, J. (1998). Myths we teach, realities we ignore: Leadership education in business schools. *The Journal of Leadership Studies*, 5(1), 82–99.

Organization for Economic Co-operation and Development. (2018). *OECD future of education and skills 2030*. Retrieved from https://www.oecd.org/education/2030-project/teaching-and-learning/learning/skills/Skills_for_2030_concept_note.pdf

Pfeffer, J. (2009). *Leadership development in business schools: An agenda for change*. Manuscript submitted for publication. Graduate School of Business, Stanford University, Stanford, CA.

Seemiller, C., & Grace, M. (2015). *Generation Z goes to college*. Hoboken, NJ: John Wiley & Sons.

Skills Gap. (2017). In *Dictionary of Business Concepts*. Retrieved from https://www.mbaskool.com/business-concepts/human-resources-hr-terms/2134-skill-gap.html

Stewart, C., Wall, A., & Marciniec, S. (2016). Mixed signals: Do college graduates have the soft skills that employers want? *Competition Forum*, 14(2), 276–281.

Swanson, R., & Holton, E., III (1997). *Human resource development research handbook: Linking research and practice*. San Francisco: Berrett-Koehler.

Tanyel, F., Mitchell, M. A., & McAlum, H. G. (1999). The skill set for success of new business school graduates: Do prospective employers and university faculty agree? *Journal of Education for Business*, 33–37.

Tulgan, B. (2018). The soft skills gap: Growing steadily from Gen X to Gen Z [Web log message]. Retrieved from https://trainingindustry.com/blog/leadership/the-soft-skills-gap-growing-steadily-from-gen-x-to-gen-z/

Tulgan, B. (2015). *Bridging the soft skills gap: How to teach the missing basics to today's young talent*. New Jersey: Jossey-Bass.

Twenge, J. M., & Foster, J. D. (2010). Birth cohort increases in narcissistic personality traits among American college students, 1982-2009. *Social Psychological and Personality Science*, 1(1), 99–106.

Vaisey, S. (2006). Education and its discontents: Over-qualification in America, 1972-2002. *Social Forces* 85(2), 835–864.

Wilhelm, W. (2002). Research on Workplace Skills Employers Want. In Wilhelm, Logan, Smith and Szul, *Meeting the Demand: Teaching "Soft" Skills*. Delta Phi Epsilon.

Williams, S. W. (2001). The effectiveness of subject matter experts as technical trainers. *Human Resource Development Quarterly*, 12(1), 91–97.

Zemke, R., Filipczak, B., & Raines, C. (2013). *Generations at work: Managing the clash of Boomers, Gen Xers, and Gen Yers in the workplace*. New York: AMACOM.

4 Ideas and Strategies for a Successful Internship Program

"Success depends upon previous preparation, and without such preparation there is sure to be failure."
Confucius

Introduction

Managing a successful internship program within a business school can depend on many factors, including the size of your staff; your student population; and the mission, vision, and values of your institution. There is no *"one-size-fits-all"* approach to developing a successful program, but there are resources and ideas that can make your program thrive regardless of any perceived barriers that you may encounter. Our outlook can have a huge impact on our success. So instead of seeing challenges, see opportunities within your college or school to effectively support the needs of your students and employers as you help open doors for more internship opportunities.

A successful internship program must involve institutional support, employer engagement, event and activity coordination, proper advising, administrative expertise, and effective course development and facilitation. We will discuss course development and facilitation in Chapter 5, but within the next few pages of this chapter, I will share ideas that you can consider as you engage in each of these areas to effectively manage your internship program. Chances are, you already have many of the tools I will mention and some of the partnerships to take your program to the next level. With a little creativity and networking, you can implement new strategies that can make your program just as effective as the next. Whether you have a well-established program, a growing program, or a new program that is still in its infancy, my hope is that you find some ideas within the pages of this chapter to help move your program even farther along.

Using Existing Institutional Technology

When I first began my work in this space, pen and paper dominated the landscape. As I became more familiar with the processes, procedures, networks, and resources available on my campus, I was able to realize how technology could revolutionize the way we administer, manage, and participate in internship programs. Gradually, I was no longer dependent on paper applications and mail delivery but was able to tap into technology to help meet my immediate needs.

During challenging times like COVID-19, technology allowed our programs to move ahead instead of fall back. COVID-19 caused many schools to quickly shift to remote learning and thousands of students lost internships while many others were forced to transition the experience to a virtual environment. Education as we know it changed dramatically, but even in the most difficult of circumstances, technology provided an ideal opportunity to learn new ways of working that can make our students more marketable as we continue to prepare them for an ever-changing workforce.

Obviously, administering an internship program can be much easier with the use of well-established internship management or career-services platforms. But unfortunately, every business school may not be in the financial position to immediately gain access to these highly respected programs in the industry. If this is your reality, that doesn't mean that you can't use existing resources at your institution to transition your program away from paper and pen and into some form of technological sophistication. In my work, I used Qualtrics to start my journey.

Qualtrics for Internship Applications

To initially transition my program to an electronic platform, I used Qualtrics. Qualtrics is a "web-based survey tool used to conduct survey research, evaluations, and other data collection activities" (Qualtrics, 2020, para. 1). While most people think of Qualtrics primarily as a survey tool, I used it as my primary application tool as well as my primary evaluation system. Qualtrics is a service made available to all faculty, staff, and students at my institution. Using some creativity, I brainstormed this question: How can I use this system to capture my student internship applications and then automatically request that the employer confirm the experience by completing an internship verification document? The term *automatic* was key.

With a small staff and large student population, it can be challenging to ensure that an appropriate, and authentic, employer confirmation is received and done so in a timely manner. Therefore, I was able to create my student application and employer confirmation forms as surveys in Qualtrics. Once the student application was created, a "trigger" was developed within the application that automatically sent an email confirmation request to whomever I desired. In my situation, I wanted an employer confirmation request form to automatically go to the employer that the student listed on his/her internship application. I also wanted a copy of the completed application to go to the student and to my office. That way, the student has no need to question whether or not the application has been received since copies are provided to both the student and the office within minutes of the application being submitted.

The most important things in this process are to ensure that application instructions are clear, and that the student provides an accurate employer or recruiter name and email address. If the student types the email address incorrectly, the employer confirmation request is not automatically submitted to the employer and the process is slowed. It is also important to make the student aware of their responsibility in ensuring that his/her supervisor receives the request if feedback from the internship office is not received within a reasonable time frame. Each form associated with the application includes an email trigger. Therefore, when the employer submits the confirmation, the student, employer, and internship office all receive copies. Students are kept in the loop throughout the process which reduces the need for follow-up inquiries to check on the status of their application. If the student has not received a follow-up from my office within a reasonable time frame, it is fair to assume that the employer or recruiter (1) did not receive the employer confirmation request or (2) it was received in his/her clutter or spam folder. Students can then follow up with the company designee to check these two things and notify our office if the form needs to be re-sent to the same or a different email address. This puts some of the responsibility back on the student and releases the office from unnecessary follow-up. It also helps to increase confidence that the employer confirmation received was completed by an actual employer and not by the student. Employers can either complete the form as it is presented or they can upload a position description to the Qualtrics portal. If they prefer not to do either, the student or employer can always email the offer letter to the internship office or connect with the office directly to submit their own internal internship forms electronically.

Qualtrics for Internship Evaluations

Qualtrics can also be used to capture and manage your academic internship course evaluations (e.g., midterm employer, employer final, and student final). Simply create your evaluations in Qualtrics as you would any other survey. To gain assurance that employer evaluations are being completed by actual employers, I connected my evaluations to what I call a "student evaluation request form" that allows students to initiate the evaluation process as part of a course assignment. In this form, students provide basic internship information (e.g. intern name, company name, supervisor name, and supervisor email address). This form is configured in advance with an email trigger that will automatically send the supervisor a direct email with a link to the appropriate evaluation and submission instructions. Once the supervisor completes the evaluation, additional email triggers allow a copy of the final evaluation to go to the student, the internship office, and the supervisor. Students are reminded to type email addresses carefully to prevent a delay in the process. Again, this helps to ensure the authenticity of the evaluations being submitted and also ensures that everyone who needs a copy, receives a copy. Qualtrics allows you to make certain questions required, allows you to download data at your convenience, and also assists you in creating professional reports with your office's internship data. As with any process, nothing is guaranteed, but this system helped a great deal in my office's ability to have confidence that what we were receiving was legitimately submitted by a supervisor at one of our employer internship sites.

All documents are received electronically in our office email account so that staff can easily sort them, as appropriate, by creating email folders that are checked daily, processed, and documented. This process also eliminates the paper trail of maintaining physical folders in a file cabinet. Saving files, later, to an electronic folder is optional since copies are automatically captured in Qualtrics, but I found it helpful considering my small staff size and large student population.

The possibilities are endless and Qualtrics is just one example of how you can collect data and manage the administrative components of your internship program if you do not have access to a career or internship management system. There may be other programs or systems at your institution that do similar things or maybe even more. Your task is to identify what they are and take time to navigate the features so that you can create something that works well for your office until you are able to advance forward into more sophisticated technology.

Qualtrics for Data Collection Procedures

Maintaining data is an important part of an internship office. Information obtained from the applications and course evaluations are excellent resources to create concise and professional reports. This data can be useful in creating reports to share with alumni, employers, prospective students, parents, and upper administration. If your internship course is not required, gathering comprehensive internship data for your entire school or college can be a challenge.

Qualtrics is also a great resource for collecting internship data across your school or college. You can configure your surveys to ensure that students are not submitting duplicate information which can aid in the accuracy of your final numbers. It can also be useful in leveling the playing field if prizes are made available as a survey completion incentive. The more data you can obtain, the more leverage you have for increased support and participation in your internship-related programs.

In 2019, Florida State University became the largest and most diverse university in the country to add experiential learning as a graduation requirement. In FSU's curriculum, experiential learning is referred to as formative experiences. These experiences involve hands-on experiences outside of the classroom like internships, service learning, undergraduate research or creative activity, international study, and significant leadership experiences (Florida State University, 2019). Perhaps participation in an internship or other form of experiential learning will become so prevalent in higher education that participation will become mandatory and data collection will become a much simpler task.

Engage with Employers

Hosting events and other activities with employers can be rewarding and challenging, depending on the size of your resources, staff, and student population. Fortunately, there are many ideas available to help you keep both your students and stakeholders engaged. Do not re-create the wheel but tap into existing resources and key colleagues that are ready to lend a helping hand. If your college or school is fortunate to have an event management team, make sure that you stay connected. They may have cost-effective resources at your disposal and can hold the key to making your events more manageable. In addition, they can help secure vendors, purchase items, and ensure that everything goes smoothly with your special event or activity.

If you have an employer engagement officer or corporate relations staff member(s), keeping employers involved and interested in your students becomes less challenging. But if you don't, that doesn't mean you can't be effective. Below are a few ideas for you to generate new connections and keep existing connections active.

1. **Tap into the resources provided by your career center.** If your internship program is part of your college's or school's career services office, employer engagement is probably not an issue. But if your academic internship function is separate from your career services office or you don't have a career services function within your college or school, you should definitely tap into this resource at the college or university level. The resources they have can be invaluable to you and your function. A career center is filled with resources that your student's need and filled with people that can help you accomplish your goal of helping your students connect with potential employers. Their employer relations staff can connect you

with potential employers through career fair participation, job boards, and more. If they are in tune with the needs of your college and the types of opportunities your students seek, they can more effectively work to identify employers and opportunities that may appeal to your student population. Your college or school can also consider developing a liaison relationship with your institution's career center. Having a career liaison tapped into the unique needs of business students can be a valuable resource for, not only, keeping employers engaged, but ensuring that your students have ample resources for their internship and career service needs.

2. **Join professional organizations.** Joining professional organizations can help you "kill two birds with one stone." While expanding your own professional network and gaining new skills, you can also connect with potential employers that may have opportunities for your students or ideas to advance your program. Most institutions encourage faculty and staff to participate in professional development opportunities and will often provide a budget to support such endeavors. Employers are often eager to learn more about your students and how they can connect. You can also share your new contact with your employer relations staff or career services team to further the recruiting relationship so that more doors can be opened for future internship and full-time employment opportunities.

Some professional development conferences may also have associated vendor showcases or career fairs that can benefit both you and your students. For example, the vendor showcase could introduce you to products and even internship programs that your students may otherwise be unaware. National MBA conferences are an excellent way to connect with potential employers. While MBA conferences target graduate students, your attendance could develop new recruiting relationships and initiate conversation about undergraduate recruiting initiatives. While the contacts you meet may not be responsible for undergraduate recruiting, they may be willing to connect you with recruiters or share additional information about opportunities that may be more appropriate for your student population. If you work with graduate students, you could take a group of students with you so they can take advantage of the career fair while you serve as a support system, connect with additional employers, and take advantage of the professional development workshops offered. Even if you go alone, your presence will allow you to network with potential employers, collect business cards, develop relationships, and share those contact with your employer relations contact back on campus. Examples of conferences with associated career fairs include, but are not limited to, the National Black MBA Association, Prospanica – The Association of Hispanic MBAs & Business Professionals, and Ascend National Association of Asian MBAs (NAAMBA) Conference & Career Exposition.

Experiential learning associations and conferences are also excellent ways to engage with colleagues and potential employers. For example, the Cooperative Education and Internship Association (CEIA) will often host virtual career fairs. Other organizations that may benefit you professionally include, but are not limited to, the National Society for Experiential Education (NSEE), the World Association of Cooperative Education (WACE), National Association of Colleges and Employers (NACE), National Business Education Association (NBEA), and the many regional affiliates associated with these organizations.

Join your local Chamber of Commerce. Some of your most valuable employers might be right in your backyard. Join your local, regional, and state Chamber of

Commerce to connect with potential employers. This is a great way to network and get the word out to potential industry partners about the talented students that you work with in your college or school. Finally, join your local chapter of the Society for Human Resource Management (SHRM). The majority of your local HR professionals are members of this organization. Go where they are, offer to present information to the group, and encourage more members and local organizations to participate in your internship initiatives. I will speak more specifically about connecting with your local business community in the coming pages of this book.

3. **Attend various types of career fairs and encourage your students to do the same.** Career fairs hosted by your college or university career center are obviously great resources to make employer connections. But what about the career fairs that may seem outside of their area of interest? If schedules allow and attendance is not restricted, go to your institution's STEM Career Fair, Communication Career Fair, or any other major specific fair that provides an opportunity to connect with potential employers. For example, a STEM career fair seems most appropriate for students in science, technology, engineering, and math, but chances are great that the recruiters representing organizations at this fair work in organizations that also hire for business-related tasks. They may be willing to share your information with a colleague or provide you information that can help you make an appropriate connection at a later time. Do your research and if potential employers that interests your students are attending other major-specific career fairs, expand your network by attending one or more of these events. Networking in all forms is helpful, even at an event that seems like an unlikely connection.

4. **Host and attend webinars and other online events with employers.** Who says you need to leave the office to make professional connections? During the COVID-19 pandemic, virtual events became more popular and necessary. Consider hosting webinars or forums to engage employers in Q&A sessions about starting and maintaining an internship program. Direct them to internal and external resources that can aid them in this process. The more effort you put into sharing information, the more supported your employers feel and more willing they may be to develop and maintain a recruiting relationship. Plus, employers with smaller budgets may jump at the opportunity to connect and learn more about how to connect with your students.

If employers or professional organizations are hosting events to engage the broader community, attend those events. Some employers may host these types of events to solicit university assistance in promoting their experiences to your student population. Not only do you learn about the experience so that you can share with the students you support, you can also share with the employers other ways they can get involved with your students for recruiting purposes. All you need is a computer and a solid Internet connection.

5. **Develop a professional mentoring program.** Employers and alumni like to make a difference in student's lives and mentoring is an excellent way to do so! Invite employers to serve as volunteer mentors. It could be as simple as developing a database of mentors that students can browse or as formal as having employers submit profiles, have students submit applications, and then work with your staff and student leaders to develop an appropriate pairing. Students could then receive specific guidelines on how to maintain an effective mentoring relationship while periodically following up with your office contact to report on the status. Essentially,

once the pairing takes place, the work of staying connected falls on the student and their mentor.

Recruit Student Ambassadors

Consider recruiting student internship ambassadors to help make your events even more special. To ensure that you get the best students on your team, create an application process that will allow students to apply for these coveted positions. Make them desirable and competitive with perks that your office can support (e.g., stipends, scholarships, collegiate swag, shirts/blazers, food, flexibility, and/or appreciation plaques or certificates at the end of their term). If financial compensation is not an option, you have several other ways to incentivize students to do their best in this role. If you select the right students, they will be your best representatives, eager to represent your office brand as they build their résumé and their own professional network.

When you select ambassadors, it is important that they receive effective training on the role, your office functions, and your overall expectations. Have them do weekly tabling sessions to share information with their peers about internships and your office resources. Let them promote your office through supervised social media posting. Allow them to share new ideas so that you can connect with students where they are online. If students are posting information on behalf of your office, ensure that posts are monitored to guarantee appropriateness. This may mean having another staff member in your office monitor their post or approve the posts before they go live.

Students can also serve as hosts for your internship events. They can accompany you to classroom visits to provide student perspectives or even represent your office themselves, when appropriate. Student ambassadors can join you on virtual workshops and maybe even host a few of their own once you feel comfortable with their training and performance. Ambassadors can serve as peer advisors if you are short-staffed with full-time internship advisors. This will allow students to share internship experiences and best practices with their peers. Host periodic panel discussions with student ambassadors about their internship experiences. The possibilities on how student ambassadors can expand your message are endless.

Host an intern mentor program that allows students to serve as peer mentors. Students that have already participated in quality internships could apply to be a peer intern mentor. Then pair less experienced students without more experienced peers. The students can expand their skills by learning from each other.

Your Local Business Community

It is amazing what you might find within your own community. Many times, especially at larger institutions, we focus much of our attention on large corporations with large budgets, and prominent programs. But do not overlook the treasures that might be right outside your door. By connecting with your local Chamber of Commerce you can easily identify and connect with small businesses, that could benefit greatly from having an intern from your institution. In turn, you can benefit from the networking, the expanded opportunities that these employers may provide, and the overall support that you might receive from their partnership. Note that support does not always need to come in the form of money. Support could be development of new internship opportunities and full-time jobs, use of space to hold events, sharing of knowledge in the form of workshops, webinars, or even classroom visits; mentoring for your students, collaboration on events, new event ideas, connections to other potential employer partners, and more. Many small businesses may need an intern but have no idea where to start in the process. The knowledge you share could be invaluable in not only helping the employer, but your students, and college as new relationships are being built. Once you make connections, you can also create events around these employers. This type of partnership may be the key to unlocking doors of opportunity that your business students and employers never knew existed.

For employers that are new to the idea of hosting an intern, you could facilitate workshops or panel discussions to share ideas and best practices. Other employers that are already successful in this area, might jump at the opportunity to sit on a panel and share ideas with peer organizations. You could host these employers on your campus and provide them with lunch or bring the event to them as a community workshop or private workshop for one company at a time. In some cases, the employer may be interested and willing to host or sponsor an event idea themselves. You can also work with your local chamber of commerce or Society for Human Resource Management (SHRM) group to host a session as part of a Chamber or SHRM event series. All they need is your expertise. Session ideas could consist of internship basics: how to start and maintain a quality internship program; and/or employer roundtable discussions to learn their perceived benefits and barriers of internship program participation. Research shows that employers play a key role in work-based learning initatives, but are seldom involved in conversations around the topic and are often unaware of the benefits they would receive from participating in an effort to strategically link education and workforce preparation (Greenfield & Stevens, 2018).

Another example could be a local employer internship recruitment fair. Local employers, small businesses, and campus partners might shy away from some university career fair events primarily because of the cost. This way, you can host a free or reduced cost career event that allows business students to connect with employers from the local or campus community . Partner with your local Chamber of Commerce to expand your reach to potential participants. Also consider hosting your event online. If there are other institutions of higher education in your community, you can maximize the impact by partnering with their business schools/colleges to create a larger event that would attract a broader audience. This could appeal more to your employer's time and resources.

If your Chamber of Commerce has a young professional's affiliate, tap into that resource as well. They host events that might appeal more to your student demographic and at times students simply are not aware. Introduce students to the groups, invite them to speak at your college, and make connections with the students that can help them get connected to the local business community while they are in school, regardless as to whether they decide to stay or leave after graduation. Students don't have to feel pressured to stay in the community after graduation, but this will give them more exposure to the business community as they gain relevant experience. At that point, they can make their own informed decisions about where they will pursue a career after graduation. It would be great for students to have a variety of experiences on their résumé as it can definitely make them more marketable upon graduation. In my community, a local employer developed what is now called the *"Job Hop."* This one-day tour gives students from the local postsecondary institutions the opportunity to visit some top businesses in the area that may be looking to hire (Access Tallahassee, 2020). "At each stop, students learn about a company's corporate culture, what type of projects they are working on, and most importantly, what types of internships and jobs are available" (Access Tallahassee, 2020, para. 1).

Finally, you can also consider packaging several of these ideas into an employer bootcamp that allows employers to go through a two-day training to learn how to start or maximize their internship program. For employers, their training could include benefits of internship participation, how to recruit within your college or school, how to set up an internship program, and how to maintain an internship program. Employers would leave with a valuable toolkit for success and a live resource that they could refer to with any questions or concerns. If you do not have the staff or time to coordinate, but you do have financial resources, you can outsource this idea to a consultant that specializes in this area. Your professional organizations, conferences, conventions, and listservs will be excellent tools to tap into these experts and their resources.

A similar program could even be developed for students that may not have internship experience, but need more information on how to get started. For students, this can include how to find an internship, how to keep an internship, benefits, preparation, goals, and networking strategies that they learn in a workshop as well as from actual networking experience from your participating employer sponsors. Make the application process competitive so that students see the prestige in the program. As the prestige increases, so will interest and more students will want to take part in your program in future semesters and years. Use program graduates as ambassadors for your next class of protegees and, as mentioned earlier, if staff and time are an issue, consider seeking a consultant to assist. You may even have alumni skilled in these areas that would be more than happy to assist free of charge. The only way to find out is to ask.

We all know the power of food so always include food, flexibility, and some type of recognition. Students and employers can earn a certificate of completion, framed award, plaque, and/or publicity on your website after successfully completing your program.

Many of the ideas that I have mentioned can be done virtually so do not let space, money, and time prevent you from hosting an amazing event that could positively impact your students and employers. It could be as simple as a virtual meet and greet for employers to meet each other to share best practices or a meet and greet for students to connect with employers that may have potential internship opportunities.

Communicate and Recognize

You could have the best, most productive internship office in the world, but if no one knows about it, how effective are you truly? Your office needs a strategy to promote your initiatives and functions to, not only the students, but other faculty and staff. Those other faculty and staff within your college can be your biggest allies or your biggest enemies. Keep them informed about your office function and they will encourage students to work with you and refer employers directly to you. Work with faculty in the college to encourage them to promote your internship office, the value of receiving academic internship credit, the value of extending invitations for classroom visits, the benefits of integrating experiential learning activities into the curriculum, and the value in collaborating with faculty and staff both in and around the college to promote career and professional development through unique learning opportunities.

Depending on your staff and college size, have staff serve as liaisons to specific majors or departments. If a department knows they have a specific person in your office to connect to for internship-related needs, it can make them feel more supported. It can also do the same for your students. For example, if you have a marketing department internship liaison, faculty and staff within that department can reach out to that liaison for workshop requests, and/or other internship related questions or concerns. If you work in a large college, it may be difficult to split internship advising by major/department. This could overwhelm some staff and underwhelm others. Students could still receive general advising from all of your staff, but if they have a concern that may be more suited for the liaison to that department, you could easily have a structure in place that advises them of the most appropriate contact for their specific internship need.

Reach out to your faculty at the beginning of each semester and offer to do a classroom visit to speak with their students. This is especially helpful if faculty are considering cancelling a class for whatever reason during the term. Encourage them to give that time to you to share some valuable internship information with the group. If you have employer partners that want to get in front of the students, this could be an excellent option for them as well. Connect with them to see if they want to attend with you so that you can share the time with each class. If they are not in your physical area, you can teleconference them into the session or perhaps you both can share virtually using various platforms like Zoom, Microsoft Teams, or Brazen, to name a few.

Also, when students and employers do something great, share the news. People love recognition but know that recognition does not always have to cost money. It could be as simple as a social media post, a personalized thank-you card, certificate, newsletter feature, a reference, or a recommendation letter. How you do it is not as important as the fact that you do it. In the following pages, I share some ideas to recognize other's accomplishments while communicating your brand to the broader audience.

1. **Office Newsletter and Social Media Posts**

    Create a periodic internship e-newsletter to share with your students. A newsletter with internship and other career content can be an excellent edition to your offerings. If you are a team of one, a weekly newsletter may be too ambitious, but this idea can easily be scaled back to biweekly or monthly. If you have the staff and/or student support, this could be an ideal task for that individual. Having a dedicated staff member for this task could create more consistency and help to ensure that the person handling this task has the writing and technical skills to produce a quality product. A graduate student could also be a great addition to your team for this role. Whoever manages this task should document procedures to make it easier to transition the task as staff transition. Your newsletter should always provide details about new internship opportunities, information on how to receive academic credit and/or recognition for the internship experience, and any internship or career related events that your office may be aware. Ensure that your newsletter is proofed before sharing.

2. **Internship Blog**

    Start an internship blog. In addition to faculty and staff, have students contribute so that you are not tasked with managing all the content and that you have diverse perspectives included. If you have the staff size, have one of your staff take the lead in managing and supervising this task. If you do not have the staff size, select a student assistant, or graduate assistant to manage this project. If you can provide a stipend, awesome! If not, note that it is still possible to get a quality student to participate. Students are always seeking opportunity to expand their resume. Plus, there are always other ways to incentivize students (e.g., food, references, recognition, etc.).

3. **Student/Employer Spotlights**

    You can also use your newsletter to feature student interns and employer supporters. This not only gives the student exposure, but it also gives exposure to internship opportunities. The frequency of your features will depend on the frequency of your newsletter and the interest of your students. You should only feature students that have given you consent to share their story. My office created a survey that we send out to our students asking if they would like to be featured in our newsletter and on our social media pages. They complete the brief survey that asks for a headshot and responses to some short questions about their internship experience. We can then use that database to pull from each week as we maintain a consistent pipeline of intern success stories to promote from our office. You can also include your college social media team on your newsletter distribution list to give your students the opportunity for even broader exposure. If your college has television screens throughout the building, feature them there. Have a special feature on your website with a new student featured each day, week, or month, to encourage other students to participate.

    Featuring students in our intern spotlight is always a great idea, but why not do an employer feature as well? Highlight some of your best intern employers in your promotional material. Do a short survey for them and ask a few questions that students would like to know. Feature them in the newsletter and on social media, with their permission, of course. Include a company photo and share your spotlight on social media. This could give your employer added exposure and help your students connect with potential employers. Highlight a mixture of small, large, local, regional, national, and global companies so that students are aware of the diversity of employers with whom you work.

4. **Create an Intern Hall of Fame**

    Create an intern hall of fame wall in or outside your office. This can also be a virtual wall on your website. Those interns that do wonderful things in their internship can be featured in your newsletter and on social media or on a formal wall with a plaque and photo. You could even create an intern of the day/week/month program where you highlight at least one intern for a designated period. Another option would be to create an application process where others nominate the students for this recognition and then your staff or designee chooses the winner(s). Nominations could be from peers, faculty, staff, employers, and even self-nominations from the student.

5. **Social Media and Text Messaging**

    Maintain a social media presence and meet students where they are. Today, that is on social media. Share student spotlights and information about your office. Consider private groups on your social media platforms to ensure that only students within your college or school can see your listings. Develop a social media plan that helps to ensure that you do not overwhelm students with posts. Explore relevant social media platforms and choose the best to meet your goals (e.g., Facebook, Twitter, LinkedIn, Instagram, etc.). A Twitter takeover, for example, will allow your office to put your Twitter account in the care of a specific individual for a designated amount of time (usually a day). During that time, your account is filled with messages that promote your office and your work. This type of activity can raise awareness for your services, increase your audience, and your engagement rate. Consult with your college's marketing department to ensure that your tactics comply with your institutions policies, and that they are utilized effectively. Maintaining a professional social media presence can be a full-time job, so again, if you don't have a dedicated staff member available to manage this task, seek supervised support from a student or graduate assistant with experience in this area.

Consider using a text messaging service to communicate with your students. Conduct a student poll to see what communication preferences they prefer. You may find that students get overwhelmed by massive amounts of emails. If text messaging is a preferred option, do not inundate students with multiple messages a day. Find an appropriate balance and vet reputable text messaging services that will provide an appropriate balance to help your faculty and staff not feel overwhelmed by the task and students by the volume of messages.

6. **Partner Appreciation Event**

    Host an occasional partner appreciation breakfast, brunch, luncheon, or dinner to thank your consistent employer supporters for all they do. Invite some of your top interns to attend and present awards to the employers while acknowledging student accomplishments . You might be able to get an employer to provide sponsorship for the event which will offset the cost to your office.

7. **Professional Development and Informational Workshops & Videos**

    If you have a professional development office/staff, partner with them to host workshops to help prepare your students for internships and beyond. Ask if you can visit their classrooms to share internship information. Collaborate to host joint sessions that allow your professional development team to present relevant topics (e.g., preparing for an internship, dress for success, résumé writing, etc.) while you talk more broadly about the benefits of an internship, how to find one, and how to gain academic credit for the experience. If your college does not have a professional development team, work with your career center to offer similar sessions. If your time will allow, host sessions yourself that you are most comfortable presenting. Coordinate with some of your employer supporters. Many would love the opportunity to get in front of your students and students would love to hear from them!

    Coordinate with your student engagement team or alumni relations staff to host a virtual or face-to-face *"Ask an Alum"* series so that students can hear directly from alums about previous internship experiences and any advice they are able to share for the student's success. This event can easily be flipped to *"Ask an Employer."* Hearing from an experienced professional can be such a benefit for a young professional. The information they share could help a student gain experience and/or provide them with an employer resource that they may not have known about prior to the session.

    Work with your academic technology staff to pre-record internship videos that can be displayed on your website, on social media, and in your course learning management system. Choose topics that are most relevant to students and employers and then solicit students and staff to serve as on-air talent for each video session. Topics of interest for students could include:

    - What is an internship and what are the benefits?
    - How do I find an internship?
    - Can I receive academic credit and pay?

- How many credit hours can I receive?
- What is academic internship credit?
- What is the application process for receiving academic credit?
- How do I make the most of my internship experience?
- How do I enroll in an academic internship course?
- What should I expect from my internship course enrollment?

   Employer topics of interest might include:

- What is an internship and what are the benefits?
- What is experiential learning and what form will work best for my company?
- Paid vs. Unpaid: Does my internship have to be paid?
- What does it mean to receive academic internship credit?
- Why should I seek an intern from your institution?
- How do I promote my internship opportunity to your students?
- How do I start a quality internship program?
- What are some tasks that my intern should be performing?
- How do I maintain a quality internship program?

If you have a college or a department skilled in this area, tap into their resources. In my role, I have been fortunate to work in a college with an academic technology team that helps me think through ideas and ultimately turn those ideas into a quality project. Employers may also need to know more about the legalities around unpaid internships. It is important that they have whatever they need to ensure that their program is up to standard and they are not violating any labor laws.

These videos could be a great resource to answer many of the questions your students or employers may have when they are unable to connect with you quickly or directly. Also, some people are visual learners so they would prefer to see you explain something if they can't get to your office or schedule a virtual meeting as opposed to learning about it in an email response or via phone. This provides an excellent way to diversify your resources for a diverse audience.

Other Events and Activities

1. **Internship Week/Month Events**
   Host an annual Internship Week or Month that emphasizes some of the other events and activities that you may host throughout the year and introduces some new activities. Ideas can include, but are not limited to, hosting an internship resource fair that brings together all of the internship resources you have on your campus; an employer panel discussion with representatives from some of your most fervent supporters; a small internship career fair that brings together employers from multiple industries; an internship contest; an awards breakfast, brunch, lunch, or dinner to recognize top intern employers and students; professional development workshops throughout the week/month; tabling activities that allow your student ambassadors to share information about your office and resources; giveaways as incentives for students that attend your events; continued publicity through social media, your website, and newsletter. Give your student ambassadors t-shirts that they can wear that say "*Ask Me About Internships*." That way, they become your walking billboard promoting your office and activities.

If you already host a collegewide or university-wide career fair, you could host a smaller internship fair that might engage more of your local business community especially if they were not able to participate in your larger event due to cost. If you have larger companies that would like to participate in the internship fair but are not able to physically visit your campus or return due to budget constraints, find out if they have any student ambassadors already on your campus that could represent them in various capacities or consider planning a virtual event that would allow employers to participate no matter the circumstances. Student ambassadors are often eager to find ways to engage with employers so they could be an ideal source for additional student/employee engagement. The possibilities are endless and depend on the duration of your event and the availability of resources. If promoted effectively and in a timely manner, you may be able to secure employers willing to sponsor your internship week/month.

Having a focused week or month on all-things *"internship"* can be a powerful statement to your students on the level of importance that internships have on their professional success. In 2017, April was designated National Internship Awareness Month (National Day , 2020). Hosting this event during April would be nice, but do not feel obligated. Your event should be planned for a week or month that works best for your students and college. For example, February worked well for me because it was close to our existing career events and early enough in the semester to assist students in their search for summer internship experiences.

2. **My Internship Experience Contest**

    If you work in a business school, I am sure that your college has an alumni board always interested in engaging with your students. If so, consider hosting an internship contest. If you have an internship course, consider adding the contest as a course assignment giving students the option to enter their assignment into the contest. Have students summarize their internship experience using either a narrated PowerPoint or video presentation. Students that opt to enter the contest will then have their presentations judged by a small group of faculty and staff. Finalist will make their presentation during one of your scheduled board meetings or a special meeting organized for this purpose. This contest can easily be held virtually to eliminate travel and other expenses that your board members could incur. Board members choose the winner(s) and provide the prizes. For example, prizes could be scholarships (e.g., $1500 first place, $1000 second place, and $500 for third place), technology-based prizes (e.g., laptop, desktop, iPad, iPhone), or service-based (e.g., professional consulting services from a board member). Give the students specific guidelines and deadline dates in advance and ensure that everyone entering the contest abides by an approved set of rules. If this is offered in an internship course, ensure that students are aware that their decision to participate or not has no bearing on their final course grade.

3. **Host a Dean's Showcase of Internship Excellence**

    This could be a spinoff from your "My Internship Experience Contest" or a completely separate event. Ask your dean's office to host a showcase of internship excellence that allows the winners and runner-ups from your contest to share their internship experiences and creative projects through poster and oral presentations. The event could include opening remarks and recognitions followed by sessions of student presentations and posters.

4. **Speed Networking**

    Host a speed networking event with your students and employer partners so that both parties can make short, meaningful connections. Speed networking can be fun, but it requires organization and structure. A designated amount of time is set for each party to interact with the other and then move on to the next person. Conversations are short, but can range from career goals and aspirations, short résumé reviews, discussions about available opportunities, and the exchange of business cards or other contact information. If students have business cards and nametags, encourage them to bring those to the event. Employers should also bring business cards and/or other promotional material that they would like to share with students.

5. **Corporate Networking**

    If speed networking is not an option or you would like to alternate activities, consider hosting a traditional corporate networking event. This is a more formal activity where students and potential employers network while enjoying hor'deourves and mocktails (the safer version of cocktails for students that may be under the legal drinking age). Always keep safety at the forefront of any event that you organize. The goal is to network so your space should not be overrun with an abundance of seating. A few high-top tables placed strategically in the room with a few chairs around the perimeter should be sufficient. If you would like, you can assign employers a high-top table to display material and then students can go from one table to the next.

6. **Tabling**

    Host tabling activities during high-traffic days in or outside of your building. My institution often hosts a weekly marketplace that consist of a medley of student activities and vendors in the student union courtyard, a high student traffic area. The popularity of this event made it an ideal location to set up a table to promote internships to the many students that would congregate in the area. Also consider doing the same directly outside of your building in a common area frequented by your students (e.g., breezeway, patio). As students enter the building, you can share information about your internship services. Tabling events can be managed by student ambassadors and/or staff and can be scheduled to take place on a weekly basis. Students love giveaways, so in addition to promotional material, provide college swag (e.g., pens, pencils, pop sockets, shirts, water bottles) and snacks. This could also be a great event to capture internship data by enticing students to complete your survey in exchange for a swag or food item. You may even have an employer partner willing to share gift cards or other company swag to include in your giveaways. Consider inviting interested employers or their brand ambassadors to physically join you during these events. Students will love it even more if they have an opportunity to connect with a potential intern employer at your table.

7. **Internship Resource Fair**

    Consider hosting an internship resource fair. You may be asking what the difference is between a resource fair and a career fair. Well, a resource fair can help you connect students with resources on your campus that can assist them in their internship search instead of connecting them directly with employers. Compile a list of all the internship resources on your campus that might be relevant to business majors. Reach out to those contacts and invite them to participate in a resource fair that could be hosted in a tabling format inside or right outside your building or done virtually. Examples of internship resources on your campus could include your college/school career services office, the university-wide career center, international programs office, global engagement office, study abroad office, and any other department on campus that may offer the opportunity for your students to participate in internships or gain meaningful insight on internship programs.

8. **On-campus Internship Program**

    Start an on-campus internship program. If one already exists, work with the coordinating office to expand opportunities for business majors. Chances are there are some untapped offices on your campus that would greatly benefit from the knowledge that a business student can bring to their office or department. Sometimes the best internship experience might be right on your own campus. This can also include virtual experiences and can be with departments outside of your college. Once these partners are identified, you can also invite them to your internship career fair and/or resource fair.

    It is always good to remember that not all students have the means to accept an internship outside of your campus environment. Reasons can include, but are not limited to, lack of transportation or limited financial resources for public transportation. Depending on the visa type, international students may have restrictions that prevent them from working off campus. Therefore, an on-campus experience can level the playing field and provide all students, regardless of circumstances, the opportunity to gain meaningful work experience.

9. **Intern Book Club**

    Start an intern book club. Develop an intern book club within an existing student organization or invite students to apply to participate every other month. They would read popular professional development books purchased by your office and participate in group discussion either virtually or in person. If you need help identifying books, tap into the expertise of your business librarian, or respected faculty members. Students are always informed of books they should read but may not be a required course component – only a recommendation. Often, they will not take the initiative on their own, but starting a book club will provide students the opportunity to expand their knowledge beyond the traditional classroom and engage in meaningful professional development conversations about topics shared from various authors. Depending on the book, you may be able to invite the author to lead the discussion or a respected alum or employer. Ngo (2020) identified the following as the 25 best business books for college students:

    - *Good to Great* by Jim Collins
    - *How to Win Friends and Influence People* by Dale Carnegie
    - *The Wealth of Nations* by Adam Smith
    - *The Big Short* by Michael Lewis
    - *Lean In* by Sheryl Sandberg
    - *Thinking, Fast and Slow* by Daniel Kahneman
    - *The 7 Habits of Highly Effective People* by Stephen R. Covey
    - *The Lean Startup: How Today's Entrepreneurs Use Continuous Innovation to Create Radically Successful Business* by Eric Ries
    - *The Innovator's Dilemma: When New Technologies Cause Great Firms to Fail* by Clayton M. Christensen
    - *The Essays of Warren Buffett* by Warren E. Buffett and Lawrence A. Cunningham

- *The Effective Executive: The Definitive Guide to Getting the Right Things Done* by Peter F. Drucker
- *In Search of Excellence: Lessons from America's Best Run Companies* by Thomas J. Peters and Robert H. Waterman Jr.
- *The Art of War* by Sun Tzu
- *The First 90 Days: Proven Strategies for Getting Up to Speed Faster and Smarter* by Michael D. Watkins
- *The Smartest Guys in the Room: The Amazing Rise and Scandalous Fall of Enron* by Bethany McLean and Peter Elkind
- *The E-Myth Revisited: Why Most Small Businesses Don't Work and What to Do about It* by Michael E. Gerber
- *The Intelligent Investor* by Benjamin Graham
- *The Fifth Discipline: The Art and Practice of the Learning Organization* by Peter M. Senge
- *Too Big to Fail: Inside the Battle to Save Wall Street* by Andrew Ross Sorkin
- *Barbarians at the Gate: The Fall of RJR Nabisco* by Bryan Burrough and John Helyar
- *The Tipping Point: How Little Things can Make a Big Difference* by Malcolm Gladwell
- *The Personal MBA: Master the Art of Business* by Josh Kaufman
- *Tribes: We Need You to Lead Us* by Seth Godin
- *Freakonomics: A Rogue Economist Explores the Hidden Side of Everything* by Steven D. Levitt and Stephen J. Dubner
- *The 4-Hour Workweek: Escape 9-5, Live Anywhere, and Join the New Rich* by Timothy Ferriss

Provide snacks, swag, or other incentives (e.g., certificates of completion, medals, etc.). Allow select students to present their takeaways in front of your board of governors at the end of the semester or year.

10. **Internship Student Organization or Club**

    Start an official internship student organization or club within your college or school. Interns (past and present) could lead your organization while recruiting other peers to join. You could even use this group as the catalyst for your student ambassador program, mentoring program, peer advising program, and book club. Poll your student population to solicit interest and then work with your student activities office to take the proper steps to become a registered student organization. This would involve selecting officers, developing guidelines, and selecting a faculty/staff advisor. In addition, the group could work with select employers on their community events. The popularity of your organization could motivate many other students to become involved which could increase the number of students that participate in an internship prior to graduation. The more prestigious the group, the better.

11. **Start a Professional Clothing Closet**

    Start a professional clothing closet in your college or school. You might be surprised how difficult it can be for some students to secure professional attire. It could be financial or simply a lack of knowledge of what is considered professional. By soliciting donations of new or gently used professional attire from faculty, staff, employers, alumni, and the community in general, you might make a world of difference in a student's life.

12. **Host a Fashion Show**

    If your students need a visual demonstration of professional attire, host a fashion show. Partner with local retailers to donate items for your students, staff, faculty, employer, or alumni to model. The retailers gain exposure for their products and you gain a potential partner in your recruitment efforts. Fashion shows can be fun and educational at the same time.

13. **Host a Business Etiquette Dinner**

    Do your students know which utensil to use and when during a business meeting? They may learn these things in your classes, but practical applications can always enhance the learning. Partner with an employer or alum to host a formal business etiquette dinner so that your students know exactly what to expect as they prepare to enter the business world.

14. **Employer and Student Listening Sessions**

    Host employer listening sessions in hopes of gathering more information on how to effectively engage them in your recruitment efforts. Chances are great that you have several employers in your local area that do not recruit interns from your college. Wouldn't it be nice to know why not? It may be as simple as they don't know how to get involved or they assume that the process is too time consuming and costly. A listening session would give you the perfect opportunity to debunk some of these myths and possibly increase your employer reach based on their needs and desires. In today's changing economy, connecting with employers must go beyond a career fair. Invite them to your college for a lunch meeting where you provide the lunch, facilitate the discussion, and answer their questions. You could also invite a more well-established employer to help facilitate and share best practices. Hearing from a peer organization can be a valuable tool.

    Also consider meeting the employers where they are. Offer to go to their place of business for an individual company meeting or ask the employer to host a group meeting on their property and then invite other employers to attend. You can even host these virtually from the comforts of your desk. Coordinate an employer webinar and invite employers to attend. Some employers may feel more comfortable speaking to you in private or responding to an anonymous survey so welcome this type of engagement as an additional option. Convenience is key so do what is best for you and your employers. Even consider mixing it up throughout the year with a combination of these formats.

    If you are having difficulty getting students involved with your office or interested in internship participation, host a student listening session. Students may not feel comfortable speaking directly to you so consider bringing in a consultant or alum, or another student to facilitate so that you get the most honest feedback possible. You might be surprised at some of the ideas that these students generate just from your desire to show them that your office cares and that you are listening. Those that don't want to participate in a listening session could have the option to share feedback anonymously via survey and those that would prefer to speak to you one-on-one could request an appointment during a time that works well for you and your staff.

15. **Provide Support for International Internship Experiences**

    Support students and their desire to intern abroad. Work with your international program's office or student travel office to coordinate activities to help student's identify international internship experiences. In addition to sharing international experiences, make sure that you work with the appropriate office to share information with students about any legal, financial, and cultural concerns they may have before pursuing and eventually participating. You should not be expected to know all the details associated with an international internship experience, but you should know the contacts at your institution that do have this information and ensure that you connect with them so that appropriate information is shared with your students. Your international programs office may introduce new experiences on a regular basis. If those experiences are related to your students, work with that office and invite representatives to speak in your classes, during special workshops, panel discussions, and even via virtual forums to ensure that questions can be asked and answers provided. Host these events throughout the year and not just on occasion. All students need support so be creative and do what you can to be of assistance. Students should be empowered to participate in these experiences if they desire and no student should feel excluded because of financial concern. Chances are great that financial resources are there; they just don't know how to tap into them. Keep them connected.

One example of a great resource for finding international and domestic experiences is GoinGlobal. GoinGlobal (2020), founded by Mary Ann Thompson over 20 years ago, uses a team of "globally-minded individuals" to personally monitor and update the career information and resources available on the site (para. 1). Features include:

- Unlimited access to more than 16 million job and internship listings.
- Location-specific career guides packed with constantly updated, expert advice on hiring trends, work permits/visa regulations, professional and social networking, culturally correct resumes/CVs, interview advice, and more.
- Expert guidelines for creating culturally correct resumes and CVs.
- A proprietary H1B visa search engine that identifies U.S. employers seeking to hire international talent.
- Corporate profiles for 450,000 key employers throughout 196 countries.
- Personal accounts that allow users to customize their career resource experience, including bookmarking and saving favorite career guides, job and internship listings, employer profiles, and H1B records.
- An analytics dashboard for account administrators that allows you to view user statistics such as overall page views, total visits, most popular page views, and most popular job keyword and location searches. (GoinGlobal, 2020, para. 6)

There are many resources available to assist your students in their international internship search. Take into consideration your student population, and the resources you have as an office. Then move forward to create some events and activities that have the potential to greatly impact your student outcomes and your employer participation!

16. **Support Your International Student Population**

Your international student population brings a wealth of knowledge and experience to your campus. However, they often experience more challenges in their employment search than other students. An international student must abide by federal regulations to legally participate in an internship. If you have an international student office with international student advisors, you should definitely connect. They will be an invaluable resource to ensure that your international business students are in compliance with all legal requirements before accepting and beginning an internship experience. While you may not be aware of all of the legal guidelines that your students face, you should, at minimum, have a partnership with an international advisor that can assist both you and the student in making this process as seamless as possible. This could be as simple as hosting joint workshops with both your career center and international student office to share pertinent information regarding their path to employment. Career staff can share job search strategies and tools that can be used within the search while your office can discuss the academic requirements for receiving academic credit for their internship experience, and your international advisor can speak to the legal requirements that international students must abide. You can also consider inviting an employment lawyer to participate in the panel or host a separate panel to elaborate on both the internship and full-time employment process. Host joint workshops throughout the semester or quarter, both in-person and virtual. Recording the session for future view is also an excellent option for those students not able to attend. Sometimes all students need is to know that you care and that you are willing to connect them with the people and resources they need. At minimum, be that connection that provides the students with valuable resources that make their internship search and overall experience a positive one.

17. **Funding and Other Resource Opportunities**

    Work with your development staff to secure funding from alums, employers, and other donors for student intern scholarship opportunities. Internship scholarships can be very helpful in supporting students that may need assistance with relocation expenses or support in paying tuition and fees for an academic internship course, especially if their internship experience is unpaid. No student should feel forced to turn down an amazing internship experience because of financial concerns. Scholarships can range in scope, type, and amount so work with your donors to determine those details and then promote to your student population. Your office can also create an Internship Fund that will allow anyone to contribute. Students can then apply for funds to cover items associated with their confirmed internship experience (e.g., relocation assistance; housing assistance; transportation while on the internship – taxi fare, bus passes, a bike; professional wardrobe; access to technology – laptop, iPad, etc.). The possibilities are endless if you are able to secure the support from your donors to make fund a reality. You will make a huge difference in the lives of so many students that otherwise might not be able to participate in the same experiences as some of their peers.

Programs that Promote Diversity and Inclusion

According to the National Association of Colleges and Employers (NACE, 2020), almost 90% of employers have a diversity recruiting strategy. While companies place a high value on building diverse and inclusive teams, Parcells (2020) found that internship programs often fall short with 30% of companies participating in an InternMatch survey reporting that their programs are not as diverse as they would like. Higher education can play a big role in changing this dynamic by offering advice and assistance to the employer they partner with so that this number can improve. Parcells (2020) offers the following for university recruiting teams that desire to change this narrative:

1. Track hiring data and diversity initiatives.
2. Expand your reach so that it includes a variety of school, locations, and organizations.
3. Invest time and money into creating mentoring programs for young students.
4. Share your diversity hiring initiatives with clear policies and goals on your website.
5. Go beyond traditional recruiting strategies and get creative (e.g., offering grants, courses, and developing more internal resources for existing employees).

As a college/school, seek out and support existing organizations that promote recruitment for diverse populations. Examples include INROADS, SEO, and MLT.

INROADS (2020a) is the "nation's largest non-profit model of salaried corporate internships and corporate and community leadership development for outstanding ethnically diverse talent at the pipeline and mid-career levels" (para. 1). INROADS (2020b) focus areas include Selection, Education Training, and Performance all of which have helped businesses access more diverse talent. Since its founding in 1970, more than 154,000 students have been placed in paid internships and over 30,000 program alumni have full-time professional and managerial positions within more than 1,000 companies (INROADS, 2020a).

SEO Career (2020) is a "free program that helps Black, LatinX, and Native American college students secure internships with partner organizations and gives them the best chance to land a return offer" (para. 3). Program participants receive interview preparation to land an internship, strategies to secure full-time offers, live instruction, online resources, exclusive events, networking, and access to top internship and full-time positions (SEO Career, 2020).

Management Leadership for Tomorrow (MLT, 2020a) is a "national nonprofit that is transforming the leadership pipelines of more than 120 leading organizations by driving breakthrough results for individuals and institutions" (para 1). The MLT (2020b) Career Prep Program helps students "gain career-accelerating skills not taught in classrooms, cultivate personal clarity, and connect with top employers for potential internship and full-time roles" (para. 2). Program highlights include 95% of Career Prep Fellows securing summer internships; 90% receiving full-time job offers prior to graduation; and 87% describing the program as "life changing" (MLT, 2020b).

Invite employers and organizations with diversity specific programs to participate in virtual and in-person information session. Host a diversity dinner, reception, networking event, or leadership and diversity day or week. As our workforce continues to change, it becomes even more important for education to support and promote these initiatives to increase the number of opportunities available to all students. As practitioners and educators, it becomes our responsibility to engage our students in varied experiences and make them aware of as many resources available as possible. To reduce any barriers to their success. It should also be our responsibility to ensure that students see themself represented in the people charged with providing them with services. Representation matters so not only consider who you are hiring when you recruit new faculty and staff, but also consider the population of students that you serve. If your under-represented students don't feel included or don't feel that they have people to connect with, they may shy away from your services; therefore, missing out on great opportunities for advancement. Create a peer mentoring program, work with your alums and employers to support diversity initiatives; or work with your campus diversity office to incorporate tactics that foster a diverse and inclusive environment. If all your students feel included, they have a much better chance at success.

Conclusion

Managing a successful internship program involves administrative skill and institutional support. While each idea in this chapter won't appeal to every internship office, it's my hope that everyone reading this text can find something that can be adapted to fit the needs of their student population. The key is to start where you are, use the resources that you have available, and push your program forward. The ultimate goal is to provide your students with the best experience possible so they are more marketable once they graduate from your institution. One person can't do this work alone, but when equipped with sufficient staff, financial resources, and the support of your college and institution as a whole, anything is possible.

References

Access Tallahassee. (2020). *Tally job hop*. Retrieved from https://accesstallahassee.com/tally-job-hop/

Florida State University. (2019). *Florida State becomes largest university to add experiential learning requirement*. Retrieved from https://news.fsu.edu/news/university-news/2019/06/13/florida-state-becomes-largest-university-to-add-experiential-learning-requirement/

GoinGlobal. (2020). *About us*. Retrieved from http://www.goinglobal.com/about

Greenfield, M, & Stevens, K. (2018). *Promising trends and challenges in work-based learning: A market scan of organizations and tools*. Retrieved from https://www.jff.org/points-of-view/promising-trends-and-challenges-work-based-learning-market-scan-organizations-and-tools/

INROADS. (2020a). *Forest T. Harper, Jr*. Retrieved from https://inroads.org/leadership/executive-leadership/forest-t-harper-jr/

INROADS. (2020b). *History & mission*. Retrieved from https://inroads.org/about-inroads/history-mission/

Management Leadership Tomorrow (MLT). (2020a). *Empowering a new generation of diverse leaders*. Retrieved from https://mlt.org/

Management Leadership Tomorrow (MLT). (2020b). *Career Prep Program*. Retrieved from https://mlt.org/career-prep/

National Association of Colleges and Employers. (2020). *Nearly 90% of employers have a diversity recruiting strategy for class of 2021*. Retrieved from https://www.naceweb.org/diversity-equity-and-inclusion/trends-and-predictions/nearly-90-percent-of-employers-have-a-diversity-recruiting-strategy-for-class-of-2021/?utm_source=spotlight-college&utm_medium=email&utm_content=txt-head&utm_campaign=content

National Day. (2020). *National internship awareness month – April*. Retrieved from https://nationaldaycalendar.com/national-internship-awareness-month-april/

Ngo, C. (2020). *The 25 best business books for college students*. Retrieved from https://www.bestcolleges.com/blog/best-business-books-college-students/

Parcells, N. (2020). *5 strategies for creating a more diverse internship program*. Retrieved from https://www.themuse.com/advice/5-strategies-for-creating-a-more-diverse-internship-program

Qualtrics. (2020). *About*. Retrieved from https://brocku.ca/information-technology/service-catalogue/hardware-and-server-support/qualtrics/

SEO Career. (2020). *Go from campus to career with SEO*. Retrieved from https://www.seo-usa.org/career/program/about/

5 Internship Courses in a Changing Environment

"The secret of change is to focus all of your energy not on fighting the old, but on building the new."
Socrates

Introduction

Internship courses are not your traditional collegiate classes. They are often administered online or in a hybrid format, are centered around an approved internship experience, and are reflective in nature. Because students are often participating in different internship experiences, assignment responses are not only reflective, but subjective. Therefore, these courses are not difficult, but when taken seriously, can be one of the most beneficial courses that a student can take during his/her academic career. Internships have the potential to lead to full-time employment and/or confirmation of one's interest in a particular field or industry. Therefore, the work devoted to reflecting on the experience can have a significant impact on a student's career decision-making process.

Internship courses, in general, should not be considered an easy way for a student to check the box for completing an elective or other graduation requirement, but practitioners have the power to develop internship course content with the potential to change the trajectory of experiential education. Unfortunately, internship courses may not take priority at all postsecondary institutions, especially those with a heavy research focus, but we have the ability to change that narrative by increasing research efforts, growing employer support, and placing more emphasis on ensuring quality in our internship course delivery. Doing this will require resources that some internship or experiential learning offices may not have. If you lack the financial and human resources necessary, these efforts may not be as robust as desired. However, if business schools continue to emphasize the importance of internships, they will need to take a hard look at their internship programs and come to the realization that if they are to truly thrive, they will require an increase in overall support. Otherwise, the quality of the course remains stagnant, declines, or never comes to fruition. Students need credible sources of motivation to take an internship seriously and that goes beyond simply finding the opportunity. Once that opportunity is secured, they need to remain engaged professionally and academically to see the full benefit of their endeavor. Regardless of where your program is now, we all have the ability to do something great with what we already have and it is my hope that some of the content in this section will allow you to do just that!

Internship courses can be offered online or face-to-face, but with the changing economy, many institutions are taking a hard look at how to deliver an effective internship course in a completely online environment. This chapter will take a look into the many components of, and available options for, a successful online internship course. In 2017, more than 6.6 million students enrolled in some form of distance education/online learning courses (Education Data, 2020). The COVID-19 pandemic highlighted the need for more improvements in online learning. More than 98% of institutions moved the majority of in-person classes online, impacting more than 3,278 schools and 22.3 million students (Education Data, 2020). At the onset of the pandemic, about 16% of employers revoked internship offers while many others postponed their experiences or moved them completely online (Hess, 2020). About 40% of employers introduced a virtual internship (Hess, 2020). "We see an incredible 42% of the U.S. labor force now working from home full-time" (Wong, 2020, para. 5).

With this new focus on working and learning remotely, it is imperative that students adapt and that postsecondary institutions prepare to ensure that quality continues despite the platform being used. Fortunately, from my experience, our internship program had been administered completely online prior to the COVID-19 pandemic. Therefore, the need to scramble to convert our existing program was nonexistent. We did, however, need to work hard to assist our students in finding virtual experiences while also assisting interested employers in converting their internships to virtual environments so that students could still gain meaningful work experience.

In this chapter, I will share some of the resources that we have used to maintain an online internship course and strategies used to make this non-traditional academic experience beneficial for the student, employer, and institution. While the ideas presented in these next few pages are based on one institution, some were developed as a result of peer feedback. I acknowledge that years of experience, research, information sharing with colleagues, and conference attendance have played a significant role in how this information has been used over the years.

It is my hope that the practitioner is able to use this as a guide to find some information that will be helpful in developing a new or enhancing an existing internship program in a virtual environment.

Instructional Delivery Methods

Depending on the institution and program type, your internship course could be delivered in one of many formats. The most common delivery methods include traditional, technology enhanced, partially online, mostly online, and fully online.

In a traditional course, instruction is delivered face-to-face. Depending on credit hours, students and instructors meet in the same space at the same time on designated day(s). This delivery method may be less common in many institutions since getting a group of interns that may be interning in different companies, cities, states, and countries together at one time on a consistent basis can be a challenge.

Technology-enhanced delivery methods are more common when the student and instructor are separated by time, space, or both. This method uses some form of technology less than 50% of the time to deliver direct instruction. In partially online delivery methods, at least 50% (or more) of the direct instruction of the course is delivered using some form of technology when the student and instructor are separated by time, space, or both. Mostly online delivery methods offer at least 80% of the direct instruction using some form of technology, and in fully online courses 100% of the direct instruction is delivered using technology (Florida State University, n.d.).

Common modes of instruction include synchronous-central, synchronous, and asynchronous. Synchonous-central requires students to participate at the same time at a centralized location. Synchronous requires students to participate at the same time from anywhere. Asynchronous requires students to participate at any time (Florida State University, n.d.). Technology-delivery indicators include web-based or Internet-based, broadcast, conferencing, materials, and mobile or portable devices. Web-based or Internet-based courses are delivered via the internet, WEB TV, video streaming on a PC, or any other Internet-based technology (Florida State University, n.d.).

The web-based asynchronous mode of instruction has been most effective in my role because of its versatility. I also find it effective for an office with a small staff and large student population that includes students in multiple majors interning in various locations and fields at different times. The examples I provide in the following pages follow this mode and delivery method; however, you should follow the mode and delivery method that works well for your institution and program. When making that decision, take into consideration your institutional type and policies, resources, and student/staff size. The samples that I provide throughout this text can be easily adapted to any delivery mode that you choose to pursue. What is most important is the quality and effectiveness of the overall course and program.

Academic Internship Course Defined

One challenge that I have often faced as a practitioner in experiential learning is how to clearly explain to students that academic internship credit is more than just having your internship verified as appropriate, but it also involves enrollment in an academic course related to the internship experience. Some student's fail to grasp the concept that simply finding the internship and having it approved by their school or college is not enough to receive academic credit for an internship experience. Once the experience is approved, students are enrolled in an accompanying course with assignments that provide a grade – pass/fail or letter grade – as part of an organized and specified program leading to a degree. It is also important that an internship course be taken simultaneously with an internship experience. The internship experience is the primary focus of the course. Therefore, students should not take the course after they have completed the internship. In my opinion, the experience should not be treated as an afterthought, but as the central focus of the internship course during that work period.

The number of credit hours received for an internship course typically depends on the institution and the number of hours the student spends working in the actual internship experience. According to the U.S. Department of Education, the credit formula is similar to that for practice credit (e.g., supervised clinical rounds, visual or performing art studio, supervised student teaching, fieldwork, etc.).

> One practice credit hour represents 304 hours per week of supervised and/or independent practice. This in turn represents between 45 and 60 hours of work per semester. Blocks of 3 practice credit hours, which equate to a studio or practice course, represent between 135 and 180 total hours of academic work per semester. (U.S. Department of Education, 2008, p. 2)

Schools vary on the number of credit hours provided for an internship course and the number of hours they require of the student to receive academic credit. Therefore, there is no right or wrong figure as long as it meets your institutional guidelines.

For example, my institution offers three-credit hour internship courses and one variable credit hour course that can be taken for 0–6 units. To qualify for a three-credit hour internship course, students must work at least 150 hours in their internship position. With the variable credit option, the number of units (or credits) taken depends on the amount of time the student spends working in the internship. For example, a student working less than the 150 hours required for our three-credit hour option would have the option to enroll in a 0-, 1-, or 2-credit hour course since they won't qualify for three units. In addition, a student taking the course for two hours may have a smaller course workload than a student enrolled for three units or credit hours. The chart below provides a sample credit hour breakdown for our variable credit hour internship course (Table 5.1).

Transcript Notation

In the previous section, I mentioned that our variable credit hour course can be taken for "0" credits (units). In this section, I will answer three of the most common questions I receive related to this option:

1. What is transcript notation?
2. Why would a student want to enroll in a zero-credit hour internship course?
3. Why would an academic department make this option available?

At my institution, students have the option to have their internship documented on their transcript through enrollment in a non-credit (0) bearing course graded pass/fail. This type of enrollment is often referred to transcript notation. While business students typically seek academic credit for their internship experience, there are times when transcript notation is necessary or considered a more appropriate option. Therefore, having this option available within your college or school can be beneficial when the need arises.

For students that participate in multiple internship experiences during their matriculation, it may not be acceptable, from an academic standpoint, to receive more than an approved amount of internship credits during their academic career. Students can always forgo the internship credit and simply document the experience on his/her

Table 5.1 Credit Hour Summary

Credit Hours	Minimum Work Hours
0	60 or more
1	90 or more
2	120 or more
3	150 or more
4	180 or more
5	210 or more
6	240 or more

résumé, but if the option exists, they can have the additional experience documented on their transcript by enrolling in a non-credit-bearing course. While the course may not provide credit, it will have some requirements that are necessary to successfully pass the course. Those requirements may include, but are not limited to (1) verification/approval of the internship, (2) a required amount of work hours, and (3) an employer final evaluation. Students enrolled in a zero-credit hour course may also be required to complete assignments (e.g., reflection paper or combination of other small reflective assignments throughout the semester). As mentioned earlier, the fewer credit hours taken will result in fewer required work hours and a lighter course workload.

Enrollment in a zero-credit hour course can also show an employer that the university supports the experience while saving the student tuition dollars if they do not need the additional academic credits. Credit hours equate to tuition costs so the more credit hours students take, the more money they spend. The zero-credit course can save the student money, provide them with transcript notation, provide an opportunity for relevant reflection, and assist the college in more accurately tracking internship participation across the entire school or college. For example, at my institution, a student can enroll in a zero-credit hour course and not be charged tuition and fees for that course if they are also enrolled in other university courses at the same time. If this is the only course the student is taking, they are charged for one-credit hour. In those cases, many students will opt to enroll in the course for one credit instead of zero since they will be charged for the one credit anyway.

Finally, a zero-credit hour option may also be beneficial for international students seeking approval for an additional internship experience during their matriculation. If they have already used the academic internship course, but have been successful in securing another internship, it may not be possible to enroll them in the same course twice. The zero-credit hour option may provide an alternative to ensure that the student continues to comply with immigration laws necessary to fulfill his/her Curricular Practical Training (CPT) requirements.

Online Internship Course Design

Structure, relevant assignments, instructor feedback, and evaluation are essential components of an online internship course. Taking a course online has advantages including being able to work on assignments at your own pace in the comfort of your home or office, and avoiding the hassle of driving to campus and searching for a parking space. However, there are some disadvantages that can also be a possibility. They include lack of interaction with the instructor and fellow participants and the lack of structure inherent in a course that meets live on a regular schedule. Therefore, it can be very easy for a student to fall behind in making normal progress toward completing the course by the end of the term. To prevent these disadvantages from taking precedent in an online internship course, it is crucial that the instructor develops a course that provides structure, flexibility, and ease in access.

Syllabi that Provide Structure

Developing a structured internship course will require a carefully planned syllabus. A syllabus provides an outline of the course content along with expectations for your course enrollment. All possible questions that a student could have about your course should have an answer available in your syllabus. Consult with your individual institution to ensure that your syllabus contains all language required by your institution. A student should be able to find what they need in this document if the instructor is not able to respond in a timely manner. A detailed syllabus is even more important when providing course content in an online format. General sections include title, term dates, course format, instructor contact information, brief course description, objectives, sample content outline, prerequisites – if necessary, grading scale, work-hour requirements, course enrollment requirements, brief overview of instructional approach, an outline of the course assignments, course drop/add policies, university attendance and academic honor policy, Americans with Disabilities Act statement, and the syllabus change policy. This document serves as your guide to developing your course content and organizing the material in your institutions learning management system.

Class Orientation

When possible, include an orientation seminar for your interns. In the age of technology, orientations can easily be done virtually. Options include recording your session in advance and posting it to your learning management system and also offering face-to-face sessions for students that are able to attend and prefer to have the option to ask questions in real time. This can also be accomplished through webinars that will allow real-time discussion and Q & A. Orientations can be a great way to ensure that your students are fully aware of the nature of your course and the expectations. I also recommend including an orientation or getting started quiz to accompany your orientation that includes true/false and multiple-choice questions. Those questions range from "do I have to pay for this course, how is this course graded, who do I contact if I have financial aid questions, to what types of assignments can I expect." There should be no guesswork in understanding the nature of your internship course. That way, you are better able to ensure that students truly understand the course expectations and design as opposed to simply trusting that they took the time to carefully review your video. By making this video readily available to students, they have a resource they can quickly refer to if you, as the instructor, are unable to respond as fast as the student would like.

To maintain a sense of connection, don't opt to only include audio in your orientation or introductory module. Students and instructors need to put names with faces. Ensure that your profile picture is visible and encourage students to include a photo in their profile as well. Something as simple as a photo can help people feel more comfortable interacting with you in a virtual environment. Do the work in advance to prepare students for the experience so that your internship course is meaningful and manageable for both you and the students.

Also consider hosting a post-internship seminar. This could be combined with your exit interview, if your office offers those experiences. Get the students together (optional or maybe even extra credit) to have a small focus group around the entire internship experience (e.g., from internship search, course enrollment, experience on the site, and experience in the course). Course evaluations are encouraged, but you may be able to receive even more detailed feedback from a formal discussion. I would offer this after grades have been posted so that no one feels as if their final grade will be affected by the feedback that they provide. You may not get a huge quorum of students, but you may get a small cohort that can provide some invaluable information to help make your courses even better for the next cohort of participants.

Grading

Internship courses can be letter graded or pass/fail. I have worked with both. To simplify both processes, I prefer to use point values based on assignment type. Points are provided for course assignments as well as evaluations using a 100-point scale. Many options exist when it comes to grading for your internship course, so use the option that works best for your program.

The A–F grading scale with accumulated point values is one option. Assignment of the final course grade is the sole responsibility of the instructor and the final grade **MUST** include the employer final evaluation. A letter-graded course plan using the point system can follow the grading plan listed below (see Table 5.2).

With the Satisfactory/Unsatisfactory (S/U) grading scale, students enrolled in a three-credit hour course must obtain at least 70 points or higher to receive a "satisfactory" grade. This total **MUST** include the employer final evaluation. Points below 70 will constitute an "unsatisfactory" final grade. If you have a variable credit hour course, the required number of points needed to pass the course will vary based on credit hours enrolled. Below is a sample syllabus excerpt for a variable credit hour internship course (0–3 credits). (See Table 5.3)

> *The Satisfactory/Unsatisfactory (S/U) grading scale is used for this course. This course is* **NOT** *letter graded so it will not affect your GPA. See chart below for a breakdown of credit hours, work hours, and point requirements. For example, students enrolled in a 3-credit hour course must obtain at least 70 points or higher to receive a "satisfactory" grade. All point totals* **MUST** *include the employer final evaluation. Failure to obtain a final employer evaluation could result in an "Incomplete or Unsatisfactory" grade.Table 5.3)*

Table 5.2 Grading Plan

Accumulated Point Range	Letter Grade
100–90	A
89–80	B
79–70	C
69–60	D
59 and below	F

Table 5.3 Point Value Summary

Credit Hour	Work Requirement	Points Required to Receive a "Satisfactory" Final Course Grade
0 - (transcript recognition/notation – GEB 4941)	60 hours or more	40 points or higher
1 - (GEB 4941)	80 hours or more	50 points or higher
2 - (GEB 4941)	100 hours or more	60 points or higher
3 - (all other internship courses)	150 hours or more	70 points or higher

Points below the values listed for each credit option will constitute an "unsatisfactory" grade. Also be reminded that the **employer final evaluation** *is still a requirement for each course enrollment option and does count toward the point values listed.*

Timelines & Flexibility

Students enrolled in an online internship course may be participating in experiences that start at different times during the semester. Therefore, flexibility is important when developing an internship course content. Everyone should be able to complete an introductory assignment at the same time since they don't typically require that the internship have already started. But for all other assignments, be prepared to have students submit those at different times depending on when their internship experience begins. Although this may be a reality for many administering an internship course, that does not mean that deadlines and timelines should not be established to more effectively manage the course. By establishing deadlines up front, there is a better likelihood that students will work hard to abide by or at least close to the deadline dates. This can prevent or reduce the influx of assignments that might be submitted during the last week(s) of the term which can overwhelm any instructor when they are trying to provide substantive feedback within a short time frame for a large cohort of students.

Establishing deadlines also helps the student plan for assignments, making the course more manageable and eliminating the need to work overtime to submit several assignments at one time at the end of the term. Establishing deadlines is a win-win for everyone. However, ensure that you make it clear to the students throughout the semester if late assignment submissions will be accepted. Students should be submitting assignments in conjunction with the work being performed in their internship. If any penalty is assessed, it should be assessed for those that have been enrolled in the course for an entire semester, but fail to submit any work until the end. Your learning management system should allow you to set deadline dates that will populate the student's learning management portal so they are reminded each time they log into the system. Establishing deadline dates benefits everyone by reducing stress in grading for instructors and increasing the likelihood of students completing tasks in conjunction with the internship experience. (See appendix for sample course outline.)

Using Modules in Your Learning Management System

Creating modules in your learning management system is an excellent way to design your course and ensure that it has a well-defined structure. Modules help to organize material into learning categories and can make it easier for everyone to stay on track. As mentioned earlier, deadline dates or timelines are key and modules can help you organize your material with associated deadline dates or timeframes. It is important to ensure that modules and assignments are aligned and that appropriate documents are uploaded and included within the appropriate section.

NACE Competencies

According to the National Association of Colleges and Employers (NACE, 2018), the following are eight competencies associated with career readiness: critical thinking/program-solving, oral/written communication, teamwork/collaboration/digital technology, leadership, professionalism/work ethic, career management, and global/intercultural fluency. Understanding these competencies can help an instructor focus their internship course content so that it fosters an environment that allows students to demonstrate these competencies through course assignment and reflection on the work being performed during the experience.

I encourage the use of these competencies in developing course assignments and module categories. In my course, I created modules that focus on the following four competencies: teamwork/collaboration, professionalism/work ethic, critical thinking/problem-solving, and oral/written communication. Instructors can easily incorporate all eight or fewer into their course content. This can depend on many factors including length of the term and credit hours received.

My module on teamwork and collaboration includes module learning objectives, a module overview of the topic, and a brief video lecture. Video lectures can be personally recorded using your institution's learning management system, you can share content from employers, or reputable platforms like LinkedIn Learning. Many institutions now have university-wide access to LinkedIn Learning, formally known as Lynda.com so check with your institution. Each module follows a similar pattern that may also include a brief quiz on the overview and lecture.

Assignments vary by module and, again, are based on the competency associated with the module. For example, the module on professionalism may include a discussion board on the characteristics of a professional while a module on ethics may include an assignment to write a personal ethics statement. I used the oral and written communication competency as the focus of my final module of the term. In this module, I asked the students to think deeply and summarize their entire internship experience, not in a reflection paper, but in a presentation. I feel that the discussion boards and other written assignments provide a great way for them to improve upon written communication skills, but I also need them to feel comfortable using technology and presenting to others. Therefore, I see the final project as the culmination of the course that gives them a break from traditional writing and lets them practice their oral communication skills in a virtual environment. Below you will find samples for modules 1–3 of an internship course administered via the Canvas Learning Management System (See Table 5.4).

Table 5.4 Sample Course Modules

Module 1: Intro/Teamwork/Collaboration (Weeks 2–3)
- **Discussion 1: Introduction & Learning Objectives**
  Due Date: XXX – Point Value: 4
Teamwork/Collaboration Overview
- **Characteristics of an Effective Team Member**
- **Quiz: Being an Effective Team Member**
  Due Date: XXX – Point Value: 4
Module 2: Professionalism (Week 4)
Characteristics of a Professional
Behavior and Business: Best Practices in Etiquette
- **Discussion 2: Characteristics of a Professional**
  Due Date: XXX – Point Value: 6
Module 3: Ethics in Business/Midterm (Weeks 5–6)
- **Writing Your Personal Ethics Statement**
  Due Date: XXX – 10 points
Midterm Evaluation
  Due date: XXX – 6 points

Assignments

An internship course should not be difficult. These courses are centered around an internship experience. Therefore, assignments should be associated with that experience. Course assignments should be relevant, straightforward, and concise. We don't want students to feel overwhelmed with "busy work," but instead we want them to see the value in each assignment as they reflect on their experience in real time. When structured properly, an internship course has the potential to be one of the most valuable courses that a student can take during their undergraduate experience.

Final reflection papers and weekly journal submissions are great ways for students to reflect on their experience. Personally, I prefer to separate a final paper or journal assignment into smaller assignments throughout the semester using the discussion board feature. Once a paper is split into smaller assignments, students are able to participate in peer discussions as they reflect on their experiences.

Interaction and Feedback in an Online Internship Course

Students are completing internships in all types of career fields so it can be very enlightening for interns to share experiences across a wide range of disciplines. In a virtual environment, this can be done in many ways including discussion board forums, course assignments, biweekly or monthly group chats using various forms of technology, and individual meetings. No student should be forced to share information in a group setting about their internship that they are uncomfortable sharing. Therefore, the instructor should ensure that students have ample opportunity to schedule individual meetings when necessary and appropriate.

Conducting an **exit interview** is also a great way for students to reflect and for you to interact with your students while gathering feedback on their overall internship and course experience. This can be done in a group setting both in person and virtually or individually depending on the number of students enrolled in your course. Choose the method that works best for you and your students. **Site visits** may not be possible if you have a small staff, small budget, and your interns are positioned all over the country. But with technology, site visits can be accomplished by scheduling electronic meetings with students and their supervisors. Programs like Zoom, Go to Meeting, Citrix, Microsoft Teams, and others provide excellent platforms to schedule quick check-in meetings with supervisors and students both individually or as a team.

As with any course, feedback is crucial, and an internship course should not be thought of any differently. When I was a student, I thrived on feedback. Therefore, you should help your students thrive as well by ensuring that they receive sufficent feedback while enrolled in your course. Internship course assignments are the instructor's way of keeping track of the student's experience. Therefore, the feedback that we provide the student based on their submissions can serve as a great support for students while they are in the field. They need to know that someone is advocating for their success and that they have a resource at the institution ready, willing, and able to support them if challenges occur.

I encourage instructors to 1) provide written assignment feedback in a timely manner; 2) when necessary, offer to schedule virtual meetings or phone calls to follow up on any issues that may concern you ; and 3) always address and celebrate the student's success when giving feedback before you address any areas for needed improvement. Hold students accountable for what they submit and how they submit. This course provides many opportunities for students to reflect and as an instructor, we should pay close attention to how effectively they are able to demonstrate that reflection. This includes attention to spelling, grammar, sentence structure, and the overall professional nature of the submission. Students should present themselves in the best light possible, not only to their employer, but to you the instructor. Make students aware if their submission does not meet professional standards. This may not always mean a deduction in points, but could possibly mean a second chance to "get it right." What better place to provide students a second chance than an internship course so that we can ensure they are fully engaged in the learning? To do this, I recommend that each assignment have a corresponding rubric. The rubric can be a vital component in ensuring that all student submissions are graded fairly and that you have an ideal space to provide feedback. In addition, it also helps if you have a teaching assistant or graduate assistant to help with the grading process. That will ensure that each person providing feedback is using the same criteria in grading.

Not having that in-person communication can be challenging, but in an online internship course, ensure that your contact information and preferred methods of communication are clear. Share weekly or biweekly course announcements with updates, reminders, and encouragement. Consider periodically posting check-in videos via your learning management system so that students can visually see you from behind the keyboard. Depending on the frequency of assignments, posting periodic videos can be helpful to further enforce this logic and help to ensure that students who may not have read the syllabus have another option to uncover relevant course information.

Reflection vs. Feedback

While feedback and reflection work together, they are different. They are "two sides of the same coin" (Education Hub, 2020, para. 1) and they complement each other in the learning process. Hattie (2011) found feedback to be one of the top 10 influences on student achievement. It can be positive or negative, but helps students move forward toward learning intentions and goals that may be challenging (Hattie, 2011). "Reflecting reminds you of what you have been thinking about, and how the ideas may connect. This process is also helpful in remembering what we have already learned" (Duplock & Hughes, 2014). "To reflect in experiential learning means to think critically about and analyze emotional responses to experiential activities in the context of course content and the learning objectives of a particular course or curriculum" (Ryerson University, 2009, para. 1).

Internship courses should be reflective in nature while providing appropriate feedback from supervisors and instructors. We typically see reflection fostered in course assignments like journal entries, discussion board posts, and final papers. Feedback, on the other hand, is given through evaluation of performance on the internship position and internship course assignments. Both are extremely important and can be fostered in several ways. The following provides an overview of nine ways to foster effective reflection in your internship course:

1. Discussion Board Forums
2. Journaling or Blogging
3. Reflection Papers
4. Video or Narrated PowerPoint Presentations

5. Ethics Statements
6. Portfolios
7. Supervisor Interview Assignments
8. Use Social Media as a Teaching Tool
9. Use Employer Evaluations as Course Assignments

When using technology and social media in your course, ensure that it meets your university standards and is a platform approved by your institution. Also ensure that it will improve your teaching while enhancing student learning.

Discussion board forums are an excellent way to engage students in online conversations. Not only are students able to see what their peers are accomplishing within their internship, but it also provides a space where students can expand their knowledge and hear new ideas that they may not have been aware of prior. Depending on the composition of your internship course, most students are not interning for the same company. Hearing multiple perspectives on various types of work can be a powerful tool in our ability to expand our learning while continually reflecting. Discussion board topics can vary, but I find great value in having students reflect on (a) learning objectives, (b) professionalism, (c) and highlights/challenges.

Establishing **learning objectives** will provide a foundation and framework for learning during your internship experience. By answering the question, "what will I accomplish as a result of this internship," students should be able to formulate at least three goals. Learning objectives should be specific and use action verbs to describe what students hope to gain from the experience. Examples include the following:

1. I will become proficient in the use of the firm's software applications.
2. I plan to study the marketing strategies used by this firm.
3. I hope to gain a better understanding of what goes into managing an insurance agency.
4. I will improve my writing and editing skills.
5. I will expand my knowledge of wealth management as a career path.
6. I will gain in-depth knowledge of office policies and procedures.
7. I will expand my professional network.

I typically format my learning objectives assignment as a discussion board post that students complete during the first week of the semester. Students are able to introduce themselves to their classmates, post at least three learning objectives, and then provide feedback to peers.

Earning and maintaining a professional reputation in the workplace is paramount for success in business. Mindtools (n.d.) identified the following six traits of a true professional:

1. Specialized Knowledge in Their Area of Expertise
2. Competency
3. Honesty and Integrity
4. Accountability
5. Self-Regulation (e.g., emotional intelligence)
6. Looking the Part (e.g., professional appearance)

In my *"Characteristics of a Professional"* discussion board assignment, I ask students to reflect on these characteristics and give examples of professionalism demonstrated at their internship site either by a supervisor, co-worker, client, or even themselves. This activity encourages the student to pay close attention to professional behaviors and develop a plan of action to improve in the area(s) they identify. As they reflect, they are often able to gather things that they may not have otherwise been aware of which makes them more intentional in their actions moving forward. The peer feedback allows them to explore areas of professionalism that their classmates may struggle with and learn from each other different strategies to improve.

In my *"Highlights and Challenges"* discussion board post, students are asked to provide feedback on their most rewarding experience, any challenges they may have experienced in their internship environment, and what they have been able to learn from those experiences. Students participate in some amazing internships and this forum allows them to share some high points and accomplishments with their peers. In the same forum, they also acknowledge that nothing is perfect and by sharing challenges, they are able to reflect on what made that experience a challenge and what can be done moving forward to improve the situation. Students should never feel forced to divulge details of their internship experience on a discussion board forum. Therefore, use this space to reflect in general, but ensure that other options are available for students to share challenges with the instructor one-on-one. This should be made clear at the beginning of your course so that students are comfortable addressing concerns with you individually whenever necessary.

Journaling is one of the most popular tools for self-reflection. Nguyen (2015) identified the following 10 benefits for keeping a journal:

1. Stretching Your IQ
2. Evoking Mindfulness
3. Achieving Goals
4. Emotional Intelligence
5. Boosting Memory and Comprehension
6. Strengthen Your Discipline
7. Improve Communication Skills
8. Healing
9. Spark Your Creativity
10. Self-Confidence

Writing a daily, weekly, or biweekly journal can be an excellent exercise to keep your students aware during their internship experience. It can be a complementary assignment in your online internship course or primary. By submitting journal assignments, students can reflect on tasks in real time which could enhance their learning.

For those that want to expand their journaling and share their thoughts with others, encourage them to blog. **Blogging** could be the start of a more long-term process of reflection that some students may grow to love.

Reflection papers gives the student an opportunity to summarize their internship experience in the form of a structured final paper. Sample sections could include an introduction, internship overview, theory to practice *(how the internship relates to their coursework)*, rewarding experiences, challenging experiences, key takeaways, and conclusion.

If writing has been a main component of your course, consider having the students reflect on their internship using a **video or a narrated PowerPoint.** Video presentations and narrated PowerPoints are a great way for students to express their creativity and improve their oral communication skills. Having good communication skills involves the ability to articulate thoughts clearly and effectively in writing and in oral forms to persons inside and outside of an organization (NACE, n.d.). Various online platforms like Kaltura, Youtube, and Vimeo can be used to record presentations and then upload to your learning management system. As always, ensure that the platform you use is approved by your institution. A narrated PowerPoint is also an excellent option for presenting a final project and can be used instead of the video presentation. This is a simple way for students to record their voice as they articulate each slide. Components of the video presentation and PowerPoint presentation could be the same as the sections in a traditional reflection paper. However, I would not recommend assigning both a reflection paper and a video/narrated PowerPoint presentation as the two assignments will appear redundant.

Ethics is defined as "the discipline dealing with what is good and bad and with moral duty and obligation" (Merriam-Webster, 2020). As students continue the learning in a practical setting, they should also be aware of the values that their internship organization shares. Have your students identify the mission, vision, and values of their internship organization and reflect on how those values align with your own. You can also consider having them write a personal and professional ethics statement that will allow them to reflect on their character, beliefs, opinions, moral, and personal philosophies so they can not only understand themselves better, but others can understand them as a person and as a professional.

Keeping a **portfolio** of their work throughout the internship experience is an excellent way to keep track of accomplishments. If the employer allows students to share samples of their work with others, students can compile this information in an electronic portfolio link that they can include on their résumé or a physical portfolio that they bring along with them during interviews and other professional meetings. If your institution or career services office has an e-portfolio system, consider using this as a first option. Confidentiality is important in any working environment so students should ensure that what they are sharing is permissible. If they are not allowed to share specific pieces of work, they can, at minimum, track the types of experiences and update their résumés to reflect their expanded skillset. Portfolios can include photos, awards, evaluations, and recommendation letters, to name a few.

Often, interns fail to connect with their supervisor in a meaningful way. Therefore, the **Supervisor Interview Assignment** will help to ensure that every intern better understands their supervisor's expectations and preferences while gaining insight into their work history and professional background. The insight provided could be extremely valuable to the student's growth and continued success in the internship position. Networking is crucial and starting with the supervisor is key.

The supervisor interview is an informational interview. Students are given an outline of potential questions and are then expected to schedule a convenient time to meet with their supervisor for a 30-minute in-person or virtual interview session. Students are expected to dress and act professionally, send a follow-up thank-you note within 24 hours of the interview session, and then submit to the instructor a summary report of what was gained from this networking experience. Students should summarize the answers provided to each question and also offer their concluding insight about the experience and what they learned. Sample questions can include, but are not limited to, the following:

1. Describe your role within the company.
2. How did you secure this position?
3. How did you get into this field?
4. What type of previous experience helped prepare you for this role (e.g., internships, previous jobs, etc.)?
5. What is the most satisfying (and least satisfying) thing about your job?
6. What type of training or education did you complete in preparation for this role? Has it helped you in this field? If not, what has?
7. What recommendations do you have for someone wanting to enter or progress in this field?

Social media has the potential to be an amazing teaching and research tool. For example, use Instagram as a way for students to reflect on their internships through images. If your college permits the use of social media as a teaching platform, encourage your student interns to share photos that reflect their typical workday. They could develop collages that document a specific workday, week, or project. With this assignment, students can creatively reflect on their experience. If the use of social media is not allowed or preferred, the same assignment can be replicated within your learning management system. Students can upload photos from their workday, week, or project using a cell phone and then reflect on what the photos represent. As always, students should abide by company confidentiality policies before sharing any written or visual information with others and instructors should abide by their institutions policies on using social media as a teaching tool.

Evaluations are crucial during an internship experience for a variety of reasons:

- Written evaluations most clearly communicate which areas of intern performance need adjustment.
- With informal, oral evaluations, interns may not remember everything the supervisor says; it's less likely interns will make the proper improvements if they can't recall all the issues they are supposed to correct.
- With written evaluations, interns can keep the progress reports and refer back to them periodically to make sure they're working toward peak performance.
- Written evaluations provide proof of supervisors' performance reviews. In the case of future disciplinary action – or if an intern is wondering why they were not invited back or offered fulltime employment – a written evaluation eliminates the intern's ability to contend, "I was never told I needed to improve in that area."
- If an intern is receiving academic credit for participation in the internship program, written evaluations should be mandatory. Getting into the habit of providing written performance evaluations for all interns simply makes an employer's program run smoother and ensures all interns are evaluated equally. (Chegg, 2020, para. 5)

The most common types of employer evaluations are the midterm and final. While your program may not require both, I highly recommend that both are incorporated into your syllabus as course assignments. A midterm evaluation helps the student know early on if they are on track for performing up to the supervisor's expectations. It also lets students know before the semester ends what areas they need to improve so they have time to do so before the experience ends. And finally, ensure that students are able to evaluate their own experiences using a student final evaluation. I consider the final employer evaluation a crucial component of the internship experience. Therefore, students are required to obtain one before they can receive a satisfactory course grade. The final evaluation is a great way to get the student's perspective on the internship as a whole and also find out in a more formal way whether the student was extended an offer to continue the internship, an offer to convert the internship to full-time, or if the student decided that they want to explore other areas. Review Chapter 4 for cost-effective ideas on how to administer your evaluations if your school doesn't use an electronic career or internship management system.

Alternative Internship Course Design

At the onset of the COVID-19 pandemic, many students lost their internship experience or had their internships postponed. For my institution, safety was a top priority. Therefore, we did not allow students to receive academic credit for an in-person experience. For students that were either required to receive academic internship credit or needed the credit to fulfill another graduation requirement, this was devastating news. Fortunately, my college was able to ensure that this policy did not negatively affect any of our students' ability to stay on track and fulfill their academic needs. To do so, we created what I call an "alternative" internship course entitled *"Learning Experientially in Business."* This course examined experiential learning concepts so that students could obtain a better understanding of the various ways to obtain experience in business and beyond. It also engaged students in meaningful reflection as they examined behaviors and situations designed to prepare them for today's competitive workforce and it was delivered 100% online. It was important for us to ensure that the learning continued even if the student was unable to participate in an actual face-to-face internship or secure a virtual internship experience. Experiential learning was a concept that many students were not familiar. They know about internships, but often fail to associate internships as a form of experiential learning. Experiential learning has long been described as the process of "learning by doing" (Kolb, 2015; Rizk, 2011) and is defined as any form of learning that allows the learner to put theory to practice (University of Texas at Austin, 2016; University of Colorado Denver, 2015). Examples of experiential learning include internships, co-ops, service learning, practicums, undergraduate research, laboratory activities, design projects, cultural immersion programs, apprenticeships, and other creative activities that provide opportunities for students to learn while doing (Moore, Barry, & Dooley, 2010; University of Colorado Denver, 2015). Other forms of experiential learning include case studies, mentorships, capstone courses, job shadowing, curriculum based on entrepreneurship, field-based consulting, and student competitions (Govekar & Rishi, 2007; Griffis, 2014; McCarthy & McCarthy, 2006).

Students were able to examine experiential learning concepts in business, recognize that experiential learning goes beyond internships, and learn how experience can be incorporated into our daily lives. Sample assignments included a detailed overview of experiential learning with an associated quiz and reflection on previously involved experiential learning activities; a case study assignment; a module on confronting bias; a module on the changing workplace; and a final module on career management and personal development. While the goal was to reinforce all types of experiential learning and to reflect on the many ways to gain experience, it was also important for us to incorporate assignments that would help our students to become more productive citizens and future employees.

Case studies allow students to use real-world situations to apply their learning. The University of Winnepeg (n.d.) noted the following:

> Rather than attempting to find a correct answer, case studies are best used to understand the opportunities and risks associated with the different ways that individuals and groups respond to particular situations. It's not practical to assume that all courses can have an out-of-classroom component built into the course design. Therefore, case studies can serve as an ideal link to experiential learning. (para. 2)

Select a case study appropriate for your student population. This could be a prepared case study that has already been published by a reputable resource or a case study submitted by one of your employer partners.

LinkedIn Learning is a valuable tool that allows individuals to expand their knowledge. With this platform, students can access 16,000+ expert-led courses, earn a certificate upon course completion, and view course material anytime on a computer or smartphone (LinkedIn Learning, 2020). For this course, it was important that students learn how to interact well with others across differences and discover how to create inclusive environments where everyone can thrive. Therefore, a LinkedIn Learning module on *Confronting Bias: Thriving Across our Differences* was incorporated into the course. After viewing the lecture, students were able to complete a short quiz and engage in reflection with peers via the discussion board forum. They also had the option to obtain certification or a badge within the LinkedIn Learning platform. Fortunately, every student at my institution was able to access this platform free of charge. Check with your institution to see if this option is available for you as well.

Another LinkedIn Learning–inspired assignment was entitled "Career Advice and Preparation." The purpose of this module was to demonstrate attitudes appropriate for career settings and to engage in reflective activities designed to influence future decisions. Students were asked to view two interviews from the LinkedIn Learning module entitled "Career Advice from Some of the Biggest Names in Business" and then asked to share what advice resonated with them most and how they plan to use that advice moving forward in their own career pursuits. As a discussion forum assignment, at least one peer response was required.

The COVID-19 pandemic changed the way we work. Therefore, an assignment entitled "The Changing Workplace: Work during and after COVID-19" was an appropriate addition to this course content. Connley, Hess, and Liu (2020) found that the coronavirus pandemic could change the way we work forever by:

1. Making work in the office a status symbol
2. Replacing meetings with email and instant messaging
3. Ending traditional business travel
4. Turning office buildings into conference centers

5. Requiring mandatory on-the-job medical screenings
6. Bringing co-workers closer
7. Making masks a wardrobe staple
8. Eliminating the standard 9–5 work schedule
9. Making home office stipends a common perk
10. Increasing workplace equity for women
11. Reducing in middle management positions
12. Accelerating automation
13. Increasing demand to close the digital divide

These potential changes warrant a closer look at the workforce of the past, present, and future. In this assignment, students were asked to interview a family member or friend currently in the workforce using a set of prepared questions to find out how COVID-19 has specifically affected the way they work. Students were then asked to provide their own personal perspective on how their career aspirations have changed as a result of the pandemic; what comments resonated most with them from their interviewee's feedback; and how they have embraced purpose, potential, perspective, and possibility during the pandemic.

Sample interviewee questions included:

1. How would you describe your place of employment and the main responsibilities of your position?
2. What have been the biggest changes in your work situation since COVID-19?
3. Of all the changes you have experienced in your work, which do you see as the most positive for you, your colleagues, and/or customers/clients?
4. Of all the changes you have experienced in your work, which do you see as the most challenging for you, your colleagues, and/or customers/clients?
5. How do you see your workplace changing after COVID-19?
6. How have you embraced purpose, potential, perspective, and possibility during COVID-19?

The culminating project included a narrated PowerPoint presentation summarizing key takeaways from the course as a whole. Other assignment options include research studies on specific forms of experiential learning, consulting projects, and virtual simulations. Nothing can truly substitute for practical work experience, but when necessary, a course of this nature can bring true value to the student's education and their quest to gain meaningful experience. Overall, the feedback that we received from student participants was positive and demonstrated how a nontraditional course can have a lasting impact on student learning. One student shared that this course was a good way to learn about experiential learning during a time when in-person internships was not an option. Another student shared that she enjoyed the engaging course delivery and found that each assignment made her think critically as she developed new skills. From this feedback, we found that the course was helpful and has the potential to become a staple within any business school curriculum. (See appendix for sample course outline.)

Conclusion

Internship courses are unlike any other courses available on a college campus. When given the attention they deserve, they can be one of the most beneficial courses your students will ever take. It certainly takes time, staff, and resources to run an internship office while facilitating an online internship course, but if your institution is invested in the important role that internships play in business education, they will support your efforts to develop and administer a course that exceeds expectations!

References

California State University Long Beach. (2020). *Qualtrics: What is Qualtrics?* Retrieved from https://csulb.libguides.com/qualtrics

Chegg. (2020). *Developing evaluation standards for your intern program.* Retrieved from https://www.internships.com/employer/resources/program/evaluations#:~:text=%20Written%20intern%20evaluations%20are%20beneficial%20for%20a,reports%20and%20refer%20back%20to%20them...%20More%20

Connley, C., Hess, A., & Liu, J. (2020). *13 ways the coronavirus pandemic could forever change the way we work.* Retrieved from https://www.cnbc.com/2020/04/29/how-the-coronavirus-pandemic-will-impact-the-future-of-work.html

Duplock, P., & Hughes, J. (2014). *Week 4: Reflection and feedback* [The Open University]. Retrieved from https://www.open.edu/openlearn/ocw/mod/oucontent/view.php?id=19238&printable=1

Education Data. (2020). *Online education statistics.* Retrieved from https://educationdata.org/online-education-statistics/

Education Hub. (2020). *Two sides of the same coin.* Retrieved from https://www.eduhub.ch/export/sites/default/files/feedback_and_reflection.pdf

Florida State University. (n.d.). *Curricular Request.* Retrieved from https://odl.fsu.edu/online-programs/development-process

Griffis, P. J. (2014). Information literacy in business education experiential learning programs. *Journal of Business & Finance Librarianship, 19,* 333–341. DOI: 10.1080/08963568.2014.952987

Govekar, M. A., & Rishi, M. (2007). Service learning: Bringing real-world education into the B-school classroom. *Journal of Education for Business, 83*(1), 3–10.

Hattie, J. (2011). *Feedback in schools.* In Douglas, K. M. & Hornsey, M. J. (Eds.), *Feedback: The communication of praise, criticism, and advice* (pp. 265–278). New York: Peter Lang Publishing, Inc.

Hess, A. (2020). *From Facebook to the state department, how coronavirus has changed summer internships.* Retrieved from https://www.cnbc.com/2020/04/24/how-internships-have-been-impacted-by-coronavirus.html

Kolb, D. A. (2015). *Experiential learning: Experience as the source of learning and development* (2nd ed). Hoboken, NJ: Pearson Education.

LinkedIn Learning. (2020). *Connect with learners in the moments that matter.* Retrieved from https://learning.linkedin.com/product-overview

McCarthy, P. R., & McCarthy, H. M. (2006). When case studies are not enough: Integrating experiential learning into business curricula. *Journal of Education for Business, 81*(4), 201–204.

Merriam-Webster. (2020). *Ethics.* Retrieved from https://www.merriam-webster.com/dictionary/ethic

Mindtools. (n.d.). *Professionalism: Developing this vial characteristic.* Retrieved from https://www.mindtools.com/pages/article/professionalism.htm

Moore, C., Barry, L. B., & Dooley, K. E. (2010). The effects of experiential learning with an emphasis on reflective writing on deep-level processing of leadership students. *Journal of Leadership in Education, 9*(1), 36–52.

National Association of Colleges and Employers. (2018). *Students: Internships positively impact competencies.*

Retrieved from https://www.naceweb.org/career-readiness/internships/students-internships-positively-impact-competencies/

National Association of Colleges and Employers. (n.d.). *Career readiness defined*. Retrieved from https://www.naceweb.org/career-readiness/competencies/career-readiness-defined/

Nguyen, T. (2015). *10 surprising benefits you'll get from keeping a journal*. Retrieved from https://www.huffpost.com/entry/benefits-of-journaling-_b_6648884

Rizk, L. (2011, May). *Learning by doing: Toward an experiential approach to professional development*. Paper presented at the meeting of the International Federation of Library Associations and Institutions, Puerto Rico.

Ryerson University. (2009). *Critical reflection- an integral component to experiential learning*. Retrieved from https://www.mcgill.ca/eln/files/eln/doc_ryerson_criticalreflection.pdf

University of Colorado Denver. (2015). *Experiential learning center*. Retrieved from http://www.ucdenver.edu/life/services/ExperientialLearning/about/Pages/WhatisExperientialLearning.aspx

University of Texas at Austin. (2016). *Experiential learning*. Retrieved from https://facultyinnovate.utexas.edu/instructional-strategies/experiential-learning

University of Winnipeg. (n.d.). *Experiential learning teaching methods*. Retrieved from https://www.uwinnipeg.ca/experiential-learning/docs/Case%20Studies.pdf

U.S. Department of Education. (2008). *Structure of the U.S. education system: Credit systems*. (International Affairs Office). Retrieved from www2.ed.gov/about/offices/list/ous/international/usnei/us/credits.doc

Wong, M. (2020). *Stanford research provides a snapshot of a new working-from-home economy*. Retrieved from https://news.stanford.edu/2020/06/29/snapshot-new-working-home-economy/

6 The Future of Business Education and Employment

"The future depends on what you do today."

Mahatma Gandhi

The Future of Business Education

The COVID-19 pandemic caused a sudden shift in education that included financial pressures, uncertainty in enrollments, pressure on the faculty and staff, and stress on the students (Kristhnamurthy, 2020). Business schools, on the other hand, were forced to handle another significant impact – the "shifting contours in the business world" (Kristhnaturhtmuty, 2020, para. 6). Krishnaumurthy (2020) noted that "as the business world changes, so should business schools" (para. 6).

Peters, Smith, and Thomas (2018) referred to the world we live in today as a "VUCA" world, one characterized by volatility, uncertainty, complexity, and ambiguity (p. 134). Globalization, technology, demographics, the knowledge economy, and the need for a sustainable planet will all contribute to more volatility in the years to come (Peters, Smith, & Thomas, 2018). But as business schools move forward, they must continue to ask three basic questions in order to thrive: (1) who teaches? (2) what do they teach? and (3) how do they teach? (Peters et al., 2018). Many other questions abound and many paths to success exist, but "the critical path is that there is alignment between the strategy and the ability to deliver on that strategy" (Peters et al., 2018, p. 147).

Elsaid and Schermerhorn (1991) identified three concepts that could help to improve the quality of today's business education: (a) reduce the number of required business courses, (b) become more innovative on the issue of curriculum integration, and (c) hire faculty from a variety of disciplines to provide a broader educational experience for the students served. Some scholars believe that business faculty lack experience in non-academic areas making it difficult for them to share knowledge from a "hands-on," more "real-world" approach (Elsaid & Schermerhorn, 1991). Classroom visits are not enough. Instead, Elsaid and Schermerhorn (1991) suggest that companies institutionalize internships to provide professional development opportunities for faculty that lack these types of experiences.

As the landscape of business education changes, schools will need to address teaching methods, research trends, and institutional structure for the discipline to thrive. Areas of teaching improvement include using real-world challenges in the classroom, blending practice and research-based faculty and topics, encouraging co-teaching, including industry professionals as guest speakers, involving students in the creation of educational content, and encouraging teamwork by incentivizing leadership and creativity (Schoemaker, 2008). Conducting long-term, team-based research could help to provide focus on specific problems that managers face on a daily basis (Schoemaker, 2008). Schoemaker (2008) found that many business issues are multifaceted requiring in-depth team research in order to be of significant value. In addition, rethinking our view of business school as more than just a place, but a "set of complex stakeholder relationships" could encourage new research and improve teaching as a whole (p. 128). While some recommendations may seem ambitious, they demonstrate the current state of business education and how globalization, distance education, and competition can influence these changes.

Globalization

Globalization is a "process of change within educational institutions extending the reach of educational engagement beyond one's home borders and deepening the richness of understanding about the increasingly global foundation of business" (AACSB International, 2011, p. 7). AACSB International (2016) has recognized globalization as an integral part of business education able to change the trajectory of the discipline. As a result, efforts to globalize business education should produce more research, better relationships and service in the profession, and more confident graduates with the competence to successfully impact business in global markets (AACSB International, 2011). According to Aggarwal (2008), the influx of technology makes globalization easier while increasing the value and availability of technological resources that are being developed across the world.

Visits to other countries, campuses on multiple continents, high percentages of foreign students, and insertion of cultural content into the curriculum are important; however, these activities alone do not justify an institution's claim that they provide a global business education (AACSB International, 2011; Schoemaker, 2008). Differences in mission and institutional environment make it difficult to prescribe a set of globalization standards that all business schools must adhere (AACSB International). Instead, those unique qualities require that each school develop a "customized approach to globalization" based on their "unique set of circumstances" (AACSB International, 2011, p. 8).

AACSB International (2011) identified the curriculum as "the most important area in which business schools should focus their globalization related efforts" (p. 25). However, the development of curriculum and teaching strategies that support globalization presents complexities that academia must address (Elsaid & Schermerhorn, 1991; Starbird & Powers, 2013). Global business education crosses multiple disciplines and involves the integration of non-business topics. Many deans find it difficult to motivate faculty to work together across disciplines and agree on teaching strategies that meet the needs of the students and faculty (Starbird & Powers, 2013). By creating a common set of goals that address the development of higher order reasoning skills and then deciding on teaching strategies that will help achieve those goals, business schools will be better equipped to implement an international business curriculum that addresses the concern for the globalization of business and management (Starbird & Powers, 2013). Zammuto (2008) found that business programs in the United States, United Kingdom, and Australia, attract over 40% of the total international enrollments. With this knowledge, it becomes imperative that faculty work together inside their unique environments to develop a consistent, comprehensive, and effective curriculum with the ability to successfully impact business development in global markets.

Distance Education

Business has been identified as the largest and most popular academic discipline in the use of distance learning to advance business education (Allen & Seaman, 2008; Zammuto, 2008).

> The terms "distance education," "online learning," and "distance learning" are often interchangeably used to describe the process of providing formal instruction to students in such a way that the instructor and the student can be separated by geography, time or both. (Mascreen, Pai P., & Pai, 2012, p. 689)

The COVID-19 pandemic completely changed the face of higher education. This once-in-a-generation global health event slowed the economy, forced stay-at-home orders, and shifted education from a traditionally face-to-face model to online instruction. Not only were faculty tasked with transitioning their courses online in a short period of time, but students lost internships, were forced to learn new technologies, and in some cases forced to leave campus and home (Krishnaumurthy, 2020). "Never in our history have entire student bodies been abruptly shifted from face-to-face to remote instruction through the use of digital technologies" (Krishnamurthy, 2020, para. 3).

Prior to COVID-19, more than half of all business schools offered distance-learning options, and annual growth in online enrollment was expected to increase more than 10% for the next decade (Curran, 2008; Zammuto, 2008). Today, distance learning is primarily universal. The delivery of educational content via the Internet saw significant growth in the late 1990s and has since become a way of life that business schools across the country have embraced. Research has shown that distance learning can be cost-effective, flexible, and equal to or superior to the learning outcomes of face-to-face delivery (Estelami, 2014).

Estelami (2014) asserted that business education has a different focus from other disciplines, requiring educators to teach skills that help organizations become more efficient, effective, and competitive. Technology has proven itself to be an effective tool for addressing various workforce concerns; therefore, business educators have been pressured to utilize distance-learning techniques to prepare future employees to handle issues that may warrant the use of such electronic means (Estelami, 2014). According to Ransdell, Kent, Gaillard-Kenney, and Long (2011), online learning allows participants to actively participate in feedback that fosters the improvement of both technical and communication skills. The sheer familiarity and convenience of technology make it a catalyst to increase faculty usage and enrollment numbers as the demand for online learning in business education increases (Zammuto, 2008). The convenience of online education could be the catalyst to increase enrollments; however, it is important that business education stay abreast of the rapidly changing technological advances that help drive this growth.

Competition

Corporate universities (or corporate training institutions) gained recognition in the 1980s when businesses began creating training and development functions to keep employees aware of the changing business environment (Rademakers, 2014; Zammuto, 2008). By the 1990s, 1600 corporate universities existed, and today that number has grown to more than 2400 (Nixon & Helms, 2002). This *do-it-yourself* approach to education has expanded, and some of the most famous examples are General Motors GM Institute, McDonald's Hamburger University, and General Electric's Crotonville. Growth in corporate universities has been linked to several reasons, including a desire to make training more systematic within the organization (Nixon & Helms, 2002) and to remain competitive in the employment space (Dillich, 2000). Companies have recognized the value that their employees bring and have invested resources into developing corporate universities that help employees work effectively within their individual organizations (Rademakers, 2014).

According to Hearn (2014), traditional colleges and universities are not threatened by the increase in corporate universities. More than 20% of the financial support that higher education receives each year comes from voluntary corporate funding (Hearn, 2014). In addition, both entities have different objectives and different competition that function within their own space (Zammuto, 2008). Many corporate universities are identified as schools, colleges, or academies operating as a functioning business unit with a specific strategic plan (Rademakers, 2014).

Objectives of corporate universities are linked to the corporation's vision and mission while the objectives of the traditional business school are linked to the institution's vision and mission. An area of future concern may include the corporate university desire to receive the same type of accreditation sought by traditional colleges and universities (Nixon & Helms, 2002).

Both educational entities serve different populations, address different needs, and have differing objectives; therefore, it is unlikely that one or the other will ever become a major threat (Zammuto, 2008). Instead, for-profit educational programs pose more of a threat to traditional business education because of their status as a "*big business*" (Zammuto, 2008). The University of Phoenix, operated by Apollo Group, is the largest for-profit institution and the largest provider of business education worldwide with revenues exceeding $2.25 billion in 2005 (Zammuto, 2008). Other large for-profit companies with institutions providing business education include Kaplan, Inc.; DeVry, Inc.; and Career Education Corporation. "Big business has already discovered business education, and it would not be easy for corporate universities to enter this market" (Zammuto, 2008, p. 259). As the need for skilled employees increases, our nation will continue to see more innovative programs that successfully merge education and industry.

Employment Outlook

According to the U.S. Bureau of Labor Statistics (2020b), "employment is projected to grow from 162.8 million to 168.8 million over the 2019–29 decade, an increase of 6.0 million jobs" (para. 1). Of the 10 occupations projected to have the most openings each year, 6 are related to the field of business – general and operations managers, project management specialists and business operations specialists, accountants and auditors, management analyst, market research analyst and marketing specialists, and personal service managers (U.S. Bureau of Labor Statistics, 2020a). According to the National Association of Colleges and Employers (2020c), the projected average salary for a 2020 business school graduate was $57,939. Management information systems had the highest average salary projection within the individual business disciplines of $63,445 while accounting was projected at $57,734 and finance projected 58,472.U.S. Department of Labor, Bureau of Labor Statistics 2020 "Employment growth in business is fueled by the expansion of existing businesses and the formation of new ones, so careers in business are very much dependent on the economy" (Watson, 2019, para 8). National Association of Colleges and Employers 2020 Graduate Management Admission Council 2019.

Between 2016 and 2017, 381,000 degrees where conferred in the field of business alone (National Center for Education Statistics, 2019). Between 1970 and 2014, the number of bachelor degrees in business tripled (Torpey, 2016). Stockwell 2014 The field of business is growing, career options are broad, and the overall employment outlook for business school graduates remains solid, demonstrating a renewed confidence in the quality of business education (Graduate Management Admission Council, 2019).

Internships and Their Role in Employment

Internships have made certain career paths more attainable for some students in post-secondary education. Throughout the years, various research studies have shown that students with internship experience are more likely to secure employment upon graduation than those without internship experience (Callahan & Benzing, 2004; D'Abate, 2010; Gault, Redington, & Schlager, 2000; Knouse, Tanner, & Harris, 1999; Knouse & Fontenot, 2008). In fact, a study by the National Association of Colleges and Employers (2020a) found that when employers have equally qualified candidates, they choose the candidate with internship experience. For interns, the offer rate was 68%, the acceptance rate was 81.6%, and the conversation rate was 55.5% (National Association of Colleges and Employers, 2020a). Retention rates are also higher for students with internship experience. Those with internal experience had a one-year retention rate of 68.7%, while those with external internship experience had a one-year retention rate of 55% (National Association of Colleges and Employers, 2020a). The five-year retention rate for intern hires with internal experience was 42.2% and 39.8% for those with external experience (National Association of Colleges and Employers, 2020a). The numbers don't lie and clearly demonstrate that internships bring value to business education and employment outcomes.

Internships During COVID-19

Vault.com has been providing career intelligence since 1996 and during the COVID-19 pandemic, they found that many employers were adapting their internship programs to meet the challenges that this health crisis brought upon the world. Of the 150 employers they surveyed in 2020, 54% converted their summer internships to fully virtual experience while 17% made part of their program virtual (Vault, 2020). Seventy-two percent of companies provided interns with necessary technology/equipment to continue their experience, while 33% of employers said that the pandemic did not affect their intention to make full-time employment offers to interns (Vault, 2020). Seventy-one percent of employers reported that the pandemic's greatest impact was the need to restructure their programs and trainings. Despite the challenges that the workforce faced as a result of COVID-19, employers appear optimistic in their hiring abilities, the impact that internships continue to have on student success, and the opportunity that it has provided to prepare employees for a more remote working environment (Vault, 2020).

Conclusion

More changes in undergraduate business education are imminent with the increasing focus on helping students gain work experience. Internships not only provide practical connections between classroom knowledge and the workplace (Hergert, 2009; Knouse & Fontenot, 2008), but they also have the ability to positively impact higher-order thinking skills such as critical thinking, decision making, and problem-solving (Griffis, 2014). With this knowledge, the growing competition in educational options, and the demands of the workforce, internships present a feasible solution to improve student outcomes.

More research is necessary to determine how to effectively implement internships into the business school curriculum (Gerken, Rienties, Giesbers, & Konings, 2012). However, Hodge, Proudford, and Holt (2014) assert that the business school of the future must first acknowledge the level of importance that experiential learning has gained in this space. In addition, they must recognize its ability to influence change in a variety of settings and situations that go beyond an individual student. Elsaid and Schermerhorn (1991) noted that for business schools to be uniquely great, they must acknowledge the past, have a vision for the future, and be open to the ideas of others. Research shows that students appreciate the benefits that internship programs provide (Hergert, 2009); however, it becomes incumbent that the institution and the employer identify and create programs that are most appropriate for the population of students being served. Despite the challenges that our world may face, business must go on and internships will continue to play a major role in that process.

References

Association to Advance Collegiate Schools of Business. (2011). *Globalization of Management Education: Changing international structures, adaptive strategies, and the impact on institutions.* Report of the AACSB International Globalization of Management Education Task Force. Retrieved from https://www.aacsb.edu/-/media/aacsb/publications/research-reports/aacsb-globalization-of-management-education-task-force-report-2011.ashx?la=en&hash=46B805416C12C419DCFEE8FC4C36DBCB3AE2519A

Association to Advance Collegiate Schools of Business. (2016). *Accreditation standards.* Retrieved from http://www.aacsb.edu/accreditation/standards

Aggarwal, R. (2008). Globalization of the world economy: Implications for the business school. *American Journal of Business, 23*(2), 5–12.

Allen, L.E., & Seaman, J. (2008). *Staying the course: Online education in the United States.* Boston, MA: The Sloan Consortium.

Callahan, G., & Benzing, C. (2004). Assessing the role of internships in the career-oriented employment of graduating college students. *Education & Training 46*(2), 82–89.

Curran, C. (2008). Online learning and the university. In W. J. Bramble & S. Panda (Eds.), *Economics of distance and online learning: Theory, Practice and Research* (pp. 26–51). New York: Routledge.

D'Abate, C. (2010). Developmental interactions for business students: Do they make a difference? *Journal of Leadership & Organizational Studies.* 17(2), 143–155.

Dillich, S. (2000, August 4). Corporate universities. *Computing Canada, 26*(16), 25.

Elsaid, H. H., & Schermerhorn, J. R. (1991). The future of higher education for business and management. *Mid-American Journal of Business, 6.2*, 11–18.

Estelami, H. (2014). The role of distance learning in business education. In Estelam (Ed.), *Frontiers of distance learning in business education* (pp. 1–10). United Kingdom: Cambridge Scholars Publishing.

Gault, J., Redington, J., & Schlager, T. (2000). Undergraduate business internships and career success: Are they related? *Journal of Marketing Education, 22*(1), 45.

Gerken, M., Rienties, B., Giesbers, B., & Konings, K. D. (2012). Enhancing the academic internship learning experience for business education – A critical review and future directions. In P. G. C. Van den Bossche, W. H. Gijselaers, R. G. Milter (Eds.), *Learning at the Crossroads of Theory and Practice (pp. 7-23)*. Heidelberg: Springer. DOI: 10.1007/978-94-007-2846-2_1

Graduate Management Admission Council. (2019). *Employability and business school graduates*. Retrieved from https://www.gmac.com/-/media/files/gmac/research/employment-outlook/employability-and-business-school-graduates_corporate-recruiters-survey-2019.pdf

Griffis, P. J. (2014). Information literacy in business education experiential learning programs. *Journal of Business & Finance Librarianship, 19*, 333–341. doi: 10.1080/08963568.2014.952987

Hearn, D. (2014. *Education in the workplace: An examination of corporate university models* [Web log message]. Retrieved from http://www.newfoundations.com/OrgTheory/Hearn721.html

Hergert, M. (2009). Student perceptions of the value of internships in business education. *American Journal of Business Education, 2*(8), 9–13.

Hodge, L., Proudford, K. L. & Holt, H. (2014). From periphery to core: The increasing relevance of experiential learning in undergraduate business education. *Research in Higher Education Journal, 26*, 1–17.

Kensing, K. (2013, July). College majors and employment trends. *CareerCast.com*. Retrieved from http://www.careercast.com/career-news/college-majors-employment-trends

Knouse, S., Tanner, J., & Harris, E. (1999). The relation of college internships, college performance, and subsequent job opportunity. *Journal of Employment Counseling, 36*(1), 35–43.

Knouse, S. B., & Fontenot, G. (2008). Benefits of the business college internship: A research review. *Journal of Employment Counseling, 45*(2), 61–66.

Krishnamurthy, S. (2020). The future of business education: A commentary in the shadow of the Covid-19 pandemic. *Journal of Business Research, 11*, 1–5. https://doi.org/10.1016/j.jbusres.2020.05.034

Mascreen, C., Pai, R. Y., & Pai, R. Y. (2012). Identifying factors for the enrollment of students towards distance education for master's course: A student's perspective. *International Journal of Digital Society, 3*(3), 689–694.

National Association of Colleges and Employers. (2020a). *Internship and co-op survey report*. Bethlehem, PA.

National Association of Colleges and Employers. (2020b). *Job Outlook*. Bethlehem, PA.

National Association of Colleges and Employers. (2020c). *Salary survey*. Bethlehem, PA.

National Center for Education Statistics. (2019). *Fast facts*. Retrieved from https://nces.ed.gov/fastfacts/display.asp?id=37

Nixon, J. C., & Helms, M. M. (2002). Corporate universities vs higher education institutions. *Industrial and Commercial Training, 34*(4/5), 144–150.

Peters, K., Smith, R. R., & Thomas, H. (2018). *Rethinking the business models of business schools: A critical review and change agenda for the future*. United Kingdom: Emerald Publishing Limited.

Rademakers, M. (2014). *Corporate universities: Drivers of the learning organization*. New York: Routledge.

Ransdell, S., Kent, B., Gaillard-Kenney, S., & Long, J.(2011). Digital immigrants fare better than digital natives due to social reliance. *British journal of educational technology, 42*, 931–938.

Schoemaker, P. J. H. (2008). The future challenges of business: Rethinking management education. *California Management Review, 50*(3), 119–139.

Starbird, S. A., & Powers, E. E. (2013). The globalization of business schools: Curriculum and pedagogical issues. *Journal of Teaching in International Business, 24*(3-4), 188–197.

Stockwell, C. (2014, October, 26). *Same as it ever was: Top 10 most popular college majors*. Retrieved from https://youthinprogress.org/documents/THE%20LOWDOWN%20FROM%20COLLEGE%20FACTUAL.PDF

Torpey, E. (2016). Business careers with high pay. *Career Outlook*, U.S. Bureau of Labor Statistics. Retrieved from https://www.bls.gov/careeroutlook/2016/article/high-paying-business-careers.htm?view_full

U.S. Department of Labor, Bureau of Labor Statistics. (2020a, October). *Education level and projected openings, 2019-29*. Retrieved from https://www.bls.gov/careeroutlook/2020/article/education-level-and-openings.htm

U.S. Department of Labor Bureau of Labor Statistics. (2020b, September, 1). *Employment projections – 2019–2029* [Pressrelease]. https://www.bls.gov/news.release/pdf/ecopro.pdf

Vault. (2020). *Navigating internships through the 2020 pandemic*. https://media2.vault.com/14339577/2020vaultemployerinternshipsreport.pdf

Watson, C. (2019). *The salary for business administration right out of college*. Retrieved from https://work.chron.com/average-salary-business-administration-major-27581.htm

Zammuto, R. F. (2008). Accreditation and the globalization of business. *Academy of Management Learning & Education*, 7(2), 256–268.

Appendices

A. Sample Internship Course Enrollment Application (online form)
B. Sample Employer Internship Confirmation (online form)
C. Sample Internship Course Syllabus
D. Sample Course Outline – Learning Experientially in Business
E. Sample Assignments and Rubrics
F. Sample Employer Midterm Evaluation (online form)
G. Sample Employer Final Evaluation (online form)

Appendix A Sample Internship Course Enrollment Application (Online Form)

1. Please select the option below that best describes your intent.
    - [Insert student categories to assist your office in properly managing each student's case (e.g., international student, student interning abroad, etc.)]
2. [Insert Terms and Guidelines Associated with Your Program]
3. By typing my name below, I acknowledge my full understanding of the terms outlined above and would like to proceed with completion of my request to receive academic credit for my internship experience. _____
4. Student's Name _____
5. Email Address_____
6. Student ID #_____
7. Current Cumulative GPA_____
8. Student Major_____
9. Classification
   __Freshman __Sophomore __Junior ___Senior __Grad Student __Non-degree-seeking
10. Please select the option that best describes your request. *[These categories will vary]*
    - I am an undergraduate student seeking enrollment in an undergraduate-level internship course for up to 3 credit hours during the semester.
    - I am an undergraduate student seeking 6 credit hours for an internship that will last more than 240 hours during the semester.
    - I am a master's student seeking enrollment in a graduate internship course for 3 credit hours during the semester.
11. Please select the course that you would like to be enrolled.
12. [Insert course name(s)]
13. What semester are you requesting internship course enrollment?
    ___Spring (year) ___Summer (year) ___Fall (year)
14. Internship Company/Organization Name_____
15. Internship City_____
16. In which state is your internship? _____
17. In which country is your internship?_____
18. What type of organization are you interning for?
    ___Public ___Private ___Non-Profit
19. Anticipated Internship Start Date _____
20. Anticipated Internship End Date _____
21. Anticipated Hours of Work Per Week (e.g., 10, 20, 40) _____
22. How did you learn about this opportunity?
    - Family or Friend
    - Professor or Advisor
    - Job Board
    - Email
    - Career Fair or other Career Event, please specify_____

23. Is this experience required for graduation?
    ___yes ___no
24. What is your expected graduation date? (Semester/Year)_____
25. Paid or unpaid?
    ___Paid ___Unpaid
26. If paid, please specify type and amount. (This information will only be used for statistical purposes.)

    - hourly _____
    - stipend _____
    - commission _____
    - other (please specify) _____

    Supervisor Information
    ***Important Note: Our office supports students working in a family-owned business; however, immediate family members should NOT serve as direct supervisors.

27. Supervisor's Name_____
28. Supervisor/Recruiter Email Address _____
    IMPORTANT: Once you submit this application, your supervisor/recruiter will automatically receive an email request to provide employer confirmation of your internship experience. Therefore, it is essential that you type his/her email address correctly to prevent delays in processing your application. If you have not been assigned a supervisor, you can provide your recruiter's name/email address instead.
29. Supervisor/Recruiter Phone Number _____
30. [Insert Student Agreement Language]
31. By typing my full name below and submitting this application, I agree to the terms and conditions outlined in this application request.
    _____

Appendix B Sample Employer Internship Confirmation (Online Form)

1. Intern Name_____
2. Intern Email Address_____
3. Company/Organization Name_____
4. Company/Organization Website Address_____
5. Company/Organization (City)_____
6. Company/Organization (Country) _____
7. Type of Organization
   ___Private Sector (for profit)
   ___Public Sector (government agency or organization)
   ___Voluntary Sector (nonprofit organization)
8. Please note that for safety reasons, we also do not permit students to work inside individual employer homes. During the current health crisis, we ask that they work remotely/virtually. If you accept this statement and agree to abide accordingly, please check yes.
   ___Yes
9. Anticipated Internship Start Date _____
10. Anticipated Internship End Date _____
11. Anticipated # of Hours Per Week _____
12. Supervisor/Recruiter Name _____
13. Supervisor/Recruiter Title _____
14. Supervisor/Recruiter Email Address _____
15. Is this a paid internship?
    ___Yes ___No
16. If paid, please choose type and amount.
    hourly rate _____
    stipend _____
    commission _____
    other (please describe) _____
17. Internship Description
18. Upload a position description here OR provide a brief description in the text box below.
19. Internship/Part-time Job Description (*if no description was uploaded above*)
    _____
    _____
    _____

20. Learning Objectives: Please list 2–3 new skills/areas of growth that the intern can expect to gain through participation in this experiential learning opportunity.
    _____
    _____
    _____

21. Confirmation and Agreement

Employer Agreement (*Please read each statement carefully and check each box to certify that you understand the terms of a traditional internship relationship.*)

___I am fully aware that this opportunity is academic in nature, and I understand that the student will be reflecting on his/her experience via an internship course administered by the College of Business.

___I agree to provide the student with some type of orientation/overview at the beginning of the internship experience.

___I agree to set goals with the student and push him/her beyond traditional administrative tasks.

___I agree to oversee the intern's work and, at minimum, provide feedback via a midterm and final evaluation provided by the College of Business. (Other arrangements can be made with employers that are only able to provide internal evaluation forms.)

___I agree to provide the student with exposure to multiple aspects of the organization.

22. Electronic Signature: I confirm that the person completing this form is the same as the supervisor name listed above, or a designated employee of the company/organization named.
    ___Yes ___No (explain below) _____
23. By typing my full name below and submitting this form, I agree that the information above is accurate and will be carried out to the best of our ability.

_____

Appendix C Sample Internship Course Syllabus Outline

[Course Title]
[Term & Dates]
[Instructor Name]
[Instructor Contact Information]

[Course Description]

The College of Business Internship Program is designed for students to gain real-world experience in their respective field through on-the-job practice. Students work under the direction of an approved industry professional and the Internship Programs Office.

[Objectives]

- Students will identify career opportunities in relevant settings.
- Students will apply skills and knowledge from the discipline in practical settings.
- Students will demonstrate attitudes appropriate for career settings.
- Students will develop and apply practical skills with projects in relevant settings.

[Sample Content]

First-Day Attendance Statement
Getting Started Quiz
Introductory Assignment/Learning Objectives
Discussion Board Assignments (multiple)
Module Quizzes
Personal Ethics Statement
Employer Midterm Evaluation
Employer Final Evaluation *(required)*
Student Final Evaluation
Final Presentation

[Prerequisites]

Students enrolled in an internship course for academic credit have met the respective department requirements for their respective course, completed an online application, and ensured submission of an employer confirmation form verifying the internship as a legitimate experiential learning opportunity. Students are responsible for securing their own internship with assistance from various resources made available by the Internship Program's Office and the university.

[Grading/Work Hours Required]

[Course Requirements]
[Mandatory Check-In Attendance]
[Assignment Submission & Due Dates]

Table 5.3 Point Value Summary

Credit Hour	Work Requirement	Points Required to Receive a "Satisfactory" final course grade
0 - *(transcript recognition/notation – GEB 4941)*	60 hours or more	40 points or higher
1 - *(GEB 4941)*	80 hours or more	50 points or higher
2 - *(GEB 4941)*	100 hours or more	60 points or higher
3 - *(all other internship courses)*	150 hours or more	70 points or higher

[Required Reading Material]
[Instructional Approach]
[Web-Enhanced Version Course]
[Learning Management System Log-in information]
[Course Announcements]
[A Note About Emails]

Table C.1 Sample Course Outline

Suggested Timeframe	Assignment Descriptions (Additional details and submission instructions are available via the course site)	Value
Week 1 [Dates]	• **Complete First Day Attendance Verification Statement** *(Failure to do so will result in you being dropped from the course.)* **(Drop/Add deadline)**	0
	• **Review Course Overview & Complete "Getting Started Quiz"** The goal of this assignment is to introduce you to the course and ensure that you understand course expectations.	6
Weeks 2–3 [Dates]	• **Discussion #1 - Introduction & Learning Objectives** This assignment will allow you to introduce yourself to the class, tell us a little about your internship organization, and establish three learning goals for your internship experience. Remember to respond to at least one peer.	4
	• **Quiz:** After viewing the video lecture on being an effective team member, take the quiz to test your knowledge. Quiz can be taken twice to ensure that you understand the concepts presented.	4
Week 4– [Dates]	• **Discussion #2 – Characteristics of a Professional** Give an example of professionalism demonstrated at your internship site either by your supervisor, a co-worker, a client, or even yourself. What area of professionalism do you need to improve upon most and what is your plan of action? Remember to respond to at least one peer.	6
Week 5–6 [Dates]	• **Writing a Personal Ethics Statement** After reviewing the course content on ethics, create your own personal ethics statement.	10
	• **Midterm Evaluation** Receiving feedback from your supervisor is crucial to your internship experience being productive; therefore, this course requires that your supervisor complete a midterm evaluation of your work performance. This evaluation can be completed electronically, but it is your responsibility to initiate the process and ensure that your supervisor receives the appropriate information in a timely manner.	6
Weeks 7–8 [Dates]	• **Discussion #3 – Internship Highlights/Challenges** What has been your most rewarding experience thus far? Have you experienced any	5

(Continued)

88 *Appendices*

Table C.1 (Continued)

Suggested Timeframe	Assignment Descriptions (Additional details and submission instructions are available via the course site)	Value
	challenges while participating in this internship? Answer at least one of the questions listed and respond to at least one peer.	
Weeks 9–10 [Dates]	• **Quiz:** After reviewing the video lectures, complete the quiz on critical thinking and problem-solving. You will be able to take this quiz twice to maximize your ability to truly understand the concepts discussed. • Catch up on course assignments. • Review guidelines for final project assignment and begin preparation for submission.	4
Weeks 11–12 [Dates]	• **Continue to prepare final project assignment** • **Student Final Evaluation** The student final evaluation gives you an opportunity to evaluate every aspect of your internship experience. This information is valuable in our ability to attract quality internship employers while delivering a quality online internship course experience for our students.	5
Weeks 13–14 [Dates]	• **Final Assignment (Bringing It All Together)** Reflect on your internship as a whole and develop either (1) a narrated PowerPoint presentation or (2) a recorded video summarizing your entire internship experience.	30
Week 15 [Dates]	• **Employer Final Internship Evaluation** The employer final internship evaluation is a comprehensive evaluation tool that allows your supervisor/mentor to provide feedback on your overall performance. It is important that we receive this document by the end of the semester and that your supervisor/mentor shares his/her thoughts with you so that you can continue to improve as you progress in your academic and professional	20
[Dates]	**Last Day of Classes** ~*Ensure that ALL course assignments/evaluations are submitted by* [Dates]	
Week 16– [Dates]	**Finals Week** *(no final exam for this course)*	
	Total Points Possible	**100**

ASSIGNMENT SUBMISSION

Note that **ALL** assignments, including employer evaluations, must be submitted by the last week of the semester even if your internship extends beyond this date. Failure to do so could result in an "Unsatisfactory" or "Incomplete" grade.

*Timeframe listed will serve as a guide. Please review [Learning Management System] for specific deadline dates.

[Course Drop/Add Policies]

[Internship Non-Completion Due to Termination or Other Employee/Employer Related Issue]
[University Attendance Policy]
[Academic Honor Policy]
[Americans with Disabilities Act]
[College of Business's Integrity Code]
[Syllabus Change Policy]

Except for changes that substantially affect implementation of the evaluation (grading) statement, this syllabus is a guide for the course and is subject to change with advance notice.

Appendix D Sample Course Outline – Learning Experientially in Business

Table D.1 Sample Course Outline – Learning Experientially in Business

Suggested Timeframe	Assignment Descriptions (Additional details and submission instructions are available via the course site)	Value
Week 1– [Dates]	**Complete First-Day Attendance Verification Statement** *(Failure to do so will result in you being dropped from the course.)*	0
	Review Course Overview	4
	• **Assignment #1:** Complete "Getting Started Quiz"	
Week 2–3 [Dates]	**Review Module 1: Experiential Learning in Business**	4

	• **Assignment #2** (Experiential Learning Quiz)
	• **Assignment #3** (Reflective Discussion):
	  a. Introduce yourself to the class (e.g., name, major, classification)
	  b. Briefly discuss the form(s) of experiential learning that you have been exposed to in your academic career (e.g., high school to present). How has that experience (or those experiences) impacted your career goals? Respond to at least one peer.	

	Assignment Objective: *To examine experiential learning concepts in business and recognize that experiential learning goes beyond internships and can be incorporated into our daily lives.*	8
Weeks 4–5 [Dates]	**Review Module 2: Case Studies**	14
	• **Assignment #4:** Review the case study entitled and respond to the corresponding questions.	
	Assignment Objective: *To apply business skills and knowledge in a virtual setting.*	
Weeks 6–7 [Dates]	**Review Module 3: Confronting Bias: Thriving Across Our Differences**	4
	• **Assignment #4 (Quiz)** • **Assignment #5 (Discussion):** What was the most insightful thing you gained from this lecture and how will it help you in confronting bias in the workplace? Post your thoughts and respond to at least one peer.	
		8

(Continued)

Table D.1 (Continued)

Suggested Timeframe	Assignment Descriptions (Additional details and submission instructions are available via the course site)	Value
Weeks 8–9 [Dates]	**Assignment Objective:** *To help participants discover how to create inclusive environments where everyone can thrive; To demonstrate attitudes appropriate for career settings.* **Review Module 4: The Changing Workplace: Work During and After COVID-19** • **Assignment #6 *(Informational Interview and Reflection)*:** Interview a family member or friend currently in today's workforce and use questions 1–6 on the informational interview worksheet to find out how COVID-19 has specifically affected the way they work. Next, answer questions 7–9 from your personal perspective. Summarize your thoughts and findings underneath each question, as appropriate. Upload the final document as a WORD or PDF file.	20
Weeks 10–11 [Dates]	**Assignment Objective:** *To engage in reflective activities designed to influence future decisions.* **Module 5: Career Advice and Preparation** • **Assignment #7: *"Career Advice from Some of the Biggest Names in Business" (LinkedIn Learning)*** – Review this module on LinkedIn Learning and choose at least two of the individual interviews posted to reflect. In the discussion board, share what advice resonated with you most and how you plan to use that advice moving forward in your own career pursuits. Respond to at least one peer. • Review guidelines for final project assignment and begin preparation for submission	8
Weeks 12–13 [Dates]	**Assignment Objectives:** *To demonstrate attitudes appropriate for career settings; to engage in reflective activities designed to influence future decisions.* • **Assignment #8: Final Project: Bringing It all Together.** Reflect on the assignments and modules that you have participated over the course of this class. Develop a narrated PowerPoint (5–7 minutes and no longer than 10 slides) discussing how can use this information to further your career plan. Presentations should include the following: introduction, review of your exposure/understanding of experiential learning, skills that the case study helped you expand, thoughts on how to prevent bias in	30

(Continued)

Table D.1 (Continued)

Suggested Timeframe	Assignment Descriptions (Additional details and submission instructions are available via the course site)	Value
Weeks 14–15 [Dates]	your future workplace, reflection on how COVID-19 has affected you and others, brief overview of your career goals, best career advice that you have ever received, overall lesson(s) learned as a result of this course. **(Due Date)** **Assignment Objectives:** *To demonstrate attitudes appropriate for career settings; to engage in reflective activities designed to influence future decisions.* • *Wrap-Up* • *Finalize final project* **(Due Date)** • *Submit any outstanding assignments* • *Complete course evaluation*	
[Dates] Week 16 [Dates]	**Last Day of Classes** **Finals Week** *(no final exam for this course)*	
	Total Points Possible	**100**

Appendix E Sample Assignments and Rubrics

Assignment #1: Introduction and Learning Objectives

This assignment will allow you to introduce yourself to the class and establish learning goals for your internship experience. Use this discussion forum to post your brief introduction and list at least three learning objectives. Next respond to at least one of your classmates.

Sample Rubric

Table E.1 Assignment #1 Sample Rubric

Criteria	Ratings			Points
Introduction Good = Introduction is clearly identified. Needs Improvement = Introduction is missing required information or no introduction provided Unsatisfactory = No introduction provided	2 Pts. (Good)	1 pt. (Needs Improvement)	0 pts. (Unsatisfactory)	
Objectives Good = Three learning objectives are clearly outlined. Needs Improvement = Learning objectives are not clear or not provided. Unsatisfactory = No introduction provided	2 Pts. (Good)	1 pt. (Needs Improvement)	0 pts. (Unsatisfactory)	
Peer Response Good = One substantive peer response is provided and it goes beyond "good luck" and/or this sounds great." Needs Improvement = Peer response lacks detail or is not provided. Unsatisfactory = No introduction provided	2 Pts. (Good)	1 pt. (Needs Improvement)	0 pts. (Unsatisfactory)	
			Total Points Possible: 6	

Assignment #2: Characteristics of a Professional

Give an example of professionalism demonstrated at your internship site either by your supervisor, a co-worker, a client, or even yourself. What area of professionalism do you need to improve upon most and what is your plan of action? After submitting your response, please respond to one of your peers.

Sample Rubric

Table E.2 Assignment #2 Sample Rubric

Criteria	Ratings			Points
Characteristic Good = Characteristic is clearly identified and described. Needs Improvement = Description is lacking in	2 Pts. (Good)	1 pt. (Needs Improvement)	0 pts. (Unsatisfactory)	

(Continued)

Table E.2 (Continued)

Criteria	Ratings			Points
detail and substance. Unsatisfactory = No introduction provided				
Peer Response Good = 1 substantive peer response is provided Needs Improvement = Peer response lacks detail Unsatisfactory = No peer response provided	2 Pts. (Good)	1 pt. (Needs Improvement)	0 pts. (Unsatisfactory)	
			Total Points Possible: 4	

Assignment #3: Personal Ethics Statement

This assignment will give you some practice in crafting your own personal ethics statement as you continue to develop yourself professionally. Please submit your ethics statement by entering the text in the box provided or uploading an MS Word or PDF file. This assignment will be graded on quality and not quantity. However, you are expected to submit a substantive assignment that demonstrates your thoughtfulness in completing this task. The following link *(link to an external site)* will provide access to tips on writing a personal ethics statement. You might also find *(XXX – sample ethics statement)* an excellent example of quality work.

Table E.3 Assignment #3 Sample Rubric

Criteria	Ratings			Points
Introduction Good = Introduction is clearly identified. Needs Improvement = Introduction is missing required information or no introduction provided Unsatisfactory = No introduction provided	2 Pts. (Good)	1 pt. (Needs Improvement)	0 pts. (Unsatisfactory)	
Objectives Good = Three learning objectives are clearly outlined. Needs Improvement = Learning objectives are not clear or not provided. Unsatisfactory = No introduction provided	2 Pts. (Good)	1 pt. (Needs Improvement)	0 pts. (Unsatisfactory)	
Peer Response Good = One substantive peer response is provided and it goes beyond "good luck" and/or this sounds great." Needs Improvement = Peer response lacks detail or is not provided. Unsatisfactory = No introduction provided	2 Pts. (Good)	1 pt. (Needs Improvement)	0 pts. (Unsatisfactory)	
			Total Points Possible: 6	

Assignment #4: Highlights and Challenges

What has been your most rewarding experience thus far? Have you experienced any challenges while participating in this internship? Answer at least one of the questions

94 *Appendices*

listed and respond to at least one peer. Your peer response should be substantive and go beyond a generic statement like "I agree" or "Great feedback."

Sample Rubric

Table E.4 Assignment #4 Sample Rubric

Criteria	Ratings			Points
Internship Highlights Good = Internship highlights/challenges are shared in an effective manner Needs Improvement = Highlights/challenges lack relevant detail Unsatisfactory = No highlights/challenges provided	2 Pts. (Good)	1 pt. (Needs Improvement)	0 pts. (Unsatisfactory)	
Peer Response Good = One substantive peer response is provided Needs Improvement = Peer response lacks detail Unsatisfactory = No peer response provided	2 Pts. (Good)	1 pt. (Needs Improvement)	0 pts. (Unsatisfactory)	
			Total Points Possible: 4	

Assignment #5: My Internship Experience: Bringing It All Together

Reflect on your internship as a whole and develop a narrated PowerPoint presentation summarizing your internship experience. The narrated PowerPoint should include the following (see detailed rubric for more specifics):

1. Introduction and Learning Objectives
2. Internship Highlights and Challenges
3. Conclusion and Final thoughts (e.g., most valuable lesson(s) thus far, etc.)

Your presentation should be at least 5–7 minutes in length and follow the detailed rubric provided. Not only will this assignment allow you to more deeply reflect, but also give you an opportunity to improve on your presentation skills as well as your use of technology. Both of these skills are essential in business and life!

Sample Rubric

Table E.5 Assignment #5 Sample Rubric

Task #	Task Title	Task	Rating
1	Introduction and Learning Objectives	• Introduce yourself: Name, Major, Classification • Describe your internship organization (e.g., organization name and service(s) provided. • Describe your specific internship duties. • Discuss the three learning objectives that you identified at the start of your internship.	8-0

(Continued)

Table E.5 (Continued)

Task #	Task Title	Task	Rating
2	Internship Highlights and Challenges	★Ensure that you include a title slide and at least one additional slide covering the information above. • Identify at least one highlight that you have experienced as a result of this internship • Identify at least one challenge that you have experienced as a result of this internship. • Explain how you have worked (or are working) to overcome the challenge. ★This section should be at least two slides in length.	6–0
3	Internship Highlights and Challenges	• Identify at least one highlight that you have experienced as a result of this internship • Identify at least one challenge that you have experienced as a result of this internship. • Explain how you have worked (or are working) to overcome the challenge. ★This section should be at least two slides in length.	6-0
4	Conclusion and Final Thoughts	• What has been the most valuable lesson you have learned, thus far, as a result of this internship? • Have you changed your long-term goals as a result of this internship? • Would you recommend this internship to other students? Why or Why not? Were you offered a full-time position or an opportunity to continue this internship into another term? ★This section should be at least two slides in length.	6-0
5	Exemplary Model of Academic Work	This presentation is an exemplary model of academic work that: • provides a coherent, reflective, thoughtful, and detailed discussion • is clearly articulated, well structured, well formatted, and demonstrates appropriate word choice • has spelling and grammatical accuracy • presentation is presented in an overall professional manner • presentation is within the 5–7-minute timing constraint provided	10-0

Comments:

Total Points: (30 points possible)

Appendix F Sample Employer Midterm Evaluation (Online Form)

1. Intern's Name_____
2. Intern's Email Address_____
3. Company Name_____
4. Supervisor's Name_____
5. Supervisor's Email Address_____
6. Date Range Evaluated_____
7. Provide one rating for each competency.

Table F.1 Sample Midterm Employer Evaluation

	Excellent	Proficient	Effective	Marginal	Unacceptable
Professional demeanor at work					
Works and communicates well with others					
Job performance					

8. Additional Comments: (If any areas require improvement, please list.)
   _____
   _____

9. I agree to share and/or discuss this evaluation with my intern. ___Yes ___No
10. I confirm that the person completing this form is the same as the supervisor name listed above.
    ___Yes ___No

Appendix G Sample Employer Final Evaluation (Online Form)

1. Intern's Name_____
2. Intern's Email Address_____
3. Company Name_____
4. Company Address_____
   City_____
5. State_____
6. Supervisor's First Name_____
7. Supervisor's
   Last Name_____
8. Supervisor's Email Address_____
9. Internship Start Date_____
10. Internship End Date_____
11. Total Hours Worked During Internship_____
12. Primary Intern Duties_____
_____
_____

13. Please evaluate the student on the following criteria:

Table G.1 Sample Employer Final Evaluation

	Excellent	Proficient	Effective	Marginal	Unacceptable
Works Well with Others					
Displays a Positive Attitude to Work					
Demonstrates Good Judgment					
Dependable					
Learns Quickly					
Produces Quality Work					
Overall Performance					

14. Attendance
    ___Regular ___Irregular

15. Punctuality
    ___Regular ___Irregular

16. In what ways can the student improve?
    _____
    _____

17. Would you be interested in another intern from our college?
    ___Yes ___No ___Maybe, please contact me in the future.

18. Any additional comments?
    _____
    _____

19. I agree to share and/or discuss this evaluation with the intern.
    ___Yes ___No

20. I confirm that the person completing this form is the same as the supervisor name listed above.
    ___Yes ___No (if no, explain below)
    _____
    _____

Thank you for completing!

Index

Note: *Italicized* page numbers refer to figures, **bold** page numbers refer to tables

70/30 principle 24

AACSB International 74
activities 47–8; on-campus internship program 46; corporate networking 45; dean's showcase of internship excellence 44; intern book clubs 46–7; international internship, support for 48–9; international students, support for 49–50; internship resource fair 45–6; internship week/month events 43–4; listening sessions 48; My Internship Experience Contest 44; scholarships, funding 50; speed networking 44–5; student organizations or clubs 47; tabling 45
Aggarwal, R. 74
Alon, I. 11
alternative internship courses 68–70
Amazon 12
American Association of University Professors (AAUP) 24
approximating 16
Ascend National Association of Asian MBAs (NAAMBA) Conference & Career Exposition 35
assignments 62–8, 66–7; blogging 65; discussion board forums 64–5; ethics 66; evaluations 67; exit interview 62; versus feedback 63–8; feedback 62–8; interaction 62–3; interactions 62–8; journaling 65; learning objectives 64; narrated PowerPoints 66; portfolio 66; reflection papers 65; sample 90–3; site visits 62; social media 67; video presentations 66
Association of Collegiate Business Schools and Programs (ACBSP) 4
Association to Advance Collegiate Schools of Business (AACSB) 2–4, 10, 11
asynchronous mode of instruction 54–5

Baby Boomers 22–3

Bennis, W.G. 12
Berg, Ivar 22
blogging 65
blogs 40–1
book clubs 46–7
bootcamps 39
Boud, D. 15
Brandt, B.L. 15–16
Buckmaster, A. 15–16
Bureau of Labor Statistics 76–7
business education: and competition 76; curriculum 4–5; future of 73–8; and globalization 74–5; history of 1–6; internships 9–17
business etiquette dinner 48

Canvas Learning Management System **61**
Cappelli, P.H. 21–2
career centers 26, 34–5
Career Education Corporation 76
career fairs 36
Carnegie Foundation 1
Chamber of Commerce 35–6, 37–9
Citrix 62
class orientation 58
clubs, joining 27
cognitive apprenticeship 15–16
cognitive skills 25
communication 26
competition 76
conferences 35
Confronting Bias: Thriving Across our Differences 69
Confucius 31
Connley, C. 69
constructivism 13
contests 44
contextual teaching and learning (CTL) 14
Cooperative Education and Internship Association (CEIA) 36

corporate networking 45
Costley, C. 15
Cottrell, C.A. 25
courses, taking 26
COVID-19 pandemic 12–13, 54, 68–70, 73, 75, 77–8
credit hours **55**, 55–6
critical thinking 26
Crotonville 76
curriculum 4–5

data collection 34
dean's showcase of internship excellence 44
DevVry Inc 76
discussion board forums 64–5
distance education 75
distance learning 75
diversity 50–2

The Education of American Businessmen (Pierson) 1
Elsaid, H.H. 73
emotional intelligence 26
emotional skills 25–6
employers: career fairs 36; engaging with 34–7; final evaluation, sample (online form) 94–5; listening sessions 48; mentoring programs 36–7; midterm evaluation, sample (online form) 94; online events 36; professional organizations 35
employment: internship's role in 77; outlook 76–7; retention rates 77
Estelami, H. 75
ethics 66
evaluations 67
exit interview 62
experiential learning 9–10, 68; benefits 10–12; internships as 9; limitations 10–12; skill development 11; as training tool 9–10

face-to-face instruction 55
fading 16
Farmer, J.A. 15–16
fashion show 48
Florida State University 34
Fontenot, G. 11
Ford Foundation 1, 4
formative experiences 34
Foster, J.D. 23
Franklin, Benjamin 9

Gaillard-Kenney, S. 75
Gault, J. 11
General Electric 76
generalizing 16
Generation Y. 11, 23
Generation Z. 22–3
globalization 12, 74–5

Go to Meeting 62
GoinGlobal 49–50
Gordon, Robert A. 1–2
Gordon-Howell Report 1–2, 4–5
grading 59
Guh, George 10
Gupta, R. 10

H1B visa 49
Halsey, V. 24
Hamburger University 76
hard skills 24
Hart Research Associates 9–10
Hearn, D. 76
Hess, A. 69
Higher Education for Business (Gordon and Howell) 1–2
high-impact practices 10
Historically Black Colleges and Universities (HBCUs) 1
Howell, James E. 1–2

inclusion 50–2
informational workshops and videos 42–3
INROADS 51
instructional delivery methods 54–5
intern book clubs 46–7
intern hall of fame 41
International Assembly for Collegiate Business Education (IACBE) 4
international internship 48–9
international internships 12–13
international students 49–50
internship courses 53–71; alternative 68–70; assignments 62–8; credit hours **55**, 55–6; definition of 55; exit interview 62; flexibility 60; interaction and feedback 62–3; modules 60–1, **61**; NACE competencies 60–1; online 57–60; overview 53–4; reflection versus feedback 63–8; site visits 62; syllabus outline, sample 84–90; timelines 60; transcript notation 56–7
internship experience contests 44
internship programs 31–52; activities 43–50; on-campus 46; diversity 50–2; employer engagement 34–7; inclusion 50–2; institutional technology in 31–4; instructional delivery methods 54–5; and local business communities 37–9; overview 31; promoting 39–43; Qualtrics 32–4; student ambassadors 37
internship resource fair 45–6
internship student organization or club 47
internship week/month events 43–4
internships 9–17; applications 32–3; benefits 10–12; cognitive apprenticeship 15–16; contextual teaching and learning 14; during COVID-19 77–8; employment confirmation, sample (online form) 83–4; enrollment

application, sample (online form) 81–3; evaluations 33; as experiential learning 9–10; as high impact practice 10; impact of 9–10; international 12–13; limitations 10–12; role in employment 77; situated learning 14–15; skill development 11; theoretical perspective 13–16; virtual 12–13; work-based learning 15

Job Hop 38
Johnson, E.B. 14
Jones, C.G. 5
journaling 65

Kaplan Inc 76
Kent, B. 75
Knouse, S.B. 11
Kolb, A.Y. 9
Kolb, D.A. 9
Krishnaumurthy, S. 73

Laker, D.R. 24
leadership skills 25–6
learning: constructivist theories of *13*, 13–16; contextual teaching and learning 14; experiential 9–12; self-directed 16; situated 14–15; work-based 15
Learning Experientially in Business 68
learning management system 60–1
learning objectives 64
Lester, S. 15
Lester, S.W. 23
LinkedIn Learning 61, 69
listening sesions 48
Liu, J. 69
local businesses 37–9
Long, J. 75
Lynda.com 61

Management Leadership for Tomorrow (MLT) 51
Marciniec, S. 24
McAlum, H.G. 24
McDonald's 76
McKibbin, L.E. 5
me-generation 23
mentoring programs 36–7
meta-cognitive skills 25
Millennials 23
Mindtools 64
Mitchell, M.A. 24
modeling 16
modules 60–1, **61**
Mukhopadhyay, K. 13
My Internship Experience Contest 44

narrated PowerPoints 66

National Association of Colleges and Employers 23
National Association of Colleges and Employers (NACE) 36, 50, 60–1, 77
National Black MBA Association 35
National Business Education Association (NBEA) 36
National Education Association 24
National Institute for Learning Outcomes Assessment 10
National Society for Experiential Education (NSEE) 36
National Survey on Student Engagement 10
Nelson, D. 25
networking 12
Nguyen, T. 65
Nichols, A.L. 25
Nirenberg, J. 25

office newsletters 40
on-campus internship program 46
online events 36
online internship courses 57–60; assignments 62–8; class orientation 58; exit interview 62; flexibility 60; grading 59; interaction and feedback 62–3; reflection versus feedback 63–8; site visits 62; syllabi 57–8; timelines 60
online learning 54, 75
Organization for Economic Co-operation and Development 25
O'Toole, J. 12

pandemic 12–13
Parcells, N. 50
partner appreciation events 42
Paul, P. 13
Peters, K. 73
Pfeffer, J. 25
physical skills 25–6
Pierson, Frank C. 1
Plato 21
Porter, L.W. 5
Porter McKibbin Report 2–5
portfolio 66
Powell, J. 24
PowerPoint 66
practical skills 25–6
problem solving 26
professional clothing closet 47–8
professional development 42–3
professional organizations, joining 35–6
Prospanica – The Association of Hispanic MBAs & Business Professionals 35

Qualtrics 32–4; for data collection 34; for

internship applications 32–3; for internship evaliations 33
Quick, J. 25

Ransdell, S. 75
Redington, J. 11
reflection: blogging 65; discussion board forums 64–5; ethics 66; evaluations 67; versus feedback 63–8; journaling 65; learning objectives 64; narrated PowerPoints 66; portfolio 66; reflection papers 65; social media 67; superior interview assignment 66–7; video presentations 66
reflection papers 65
retention rates 77
Rosenstein, A. 10
Rothman, M. 10
rubrics, sample 90–3

Schermerhorn, J.R. 73
Schlager, T. 11
Schoemaker, P.J.H. 74
scholarships 50
Schultz, N.J. 23
self-control 26
self-directed learning 16
SEO Career 51
Sisman, R. 10
site visits 62
situated learning 14–15
skill development 26–7
skills gap 21–8; in college graduates 21; curriculum reform for 24; employer perception of 24; generational impact of 22–3; hard skills 24; overview 21–2; reasons for 21; skill development 26–7; skills for the future 23–6; soft skills 22, 24; soft skills 21
Smith, R.R. 73
social media 40, 41–2, 67
social skills 25–6
social-cultural process 14
Society for Human Resource Management (SHRM) 36, 38
Society of Human Resource Management 24
Socrates 53
soft skills 21, 22; soft skills 24
Solomon, N. 15
speed networking 44–5
Standifer, R.L. 23
STEM career fair 36

Stewart, C. 24
student ambassadors 37
student organizations or clubs 47
student/employer spotlights 41
superior interview assignment 66–7
Sweeney, C. 10
syllabi 57–8
Symes, C. 15
synchronous mode of instruction 55
synchronous-central mode of instruction 55

tabling 45
Tanyel, F. 24
teamwork 26
technological competence 26
text messaging 41–2
Thomas, H. 73
Thompson, Mary Ann 49–50
transcript notation 56–7
Tulgan, B. 22, 23
Twenge, J.M. 23
Twitter 41–2

University of Pennsylvania 1
University of Phoenix 76

Vaisey, S. 22
video presentations 66
videos 42–3
virtual internships 12–13
volunteering 26
Vriens, M. 12

Wall, A. 24
web-based instruction 55
webinars 36
Weihenmayer, Erik 21
Wharton School 1
Windsor, J.M. 23
work-based learning 15
workshops 42–3
World Association of Cooperative Education (WACE) 36

Zammuto, R.F. 74–5
zero-credit hour course 57
Zhang, F. 12
Zoom 62

Printed in the United States
by Baker & Taylor Publisher Services